Wealth-Blessed

Why Good People Lose Everything—
And Why You Don't Have To

Elizabeth Brickman

Praise *for* Wealth-Blessed

"Elizabeth Brickman is a beacon of wisdom in the world of biblical finance, combining her expertise as a Certified Kingdom Advisor® with a heart devoted to helping others achieve Christ-centered success. Her guidance empowers believers to approach finances with faith, purpose, and a commitment to Kingdom generosity."

– **Rob West**, CEO, Kingdom Advisors, & Host of the Nationally Syndicated Radio Show, *Faith & Finance*

"The world is a better place because of Elizabeth Brickman. What a heart! Her ability to bring faith and finance together in practical and spiritual ways is a gift!"

– **Bob Doll**, CEO/CIO, Crossmark Global Investments

"I respect Elizabeth Brickman for her knowledge, her heart, and her focus on encouraging people to have a stronger, happier relationship with God and with money. Elizabeth exemplifies servant-leadership."

– **Ginger Martin**, President & CEO, American National Bank, Broward County's oldest and largest community bank, and Federal Reserve Bank of Atlanta, Miami Branch Board of Directors

"Elizabeth lives and loves generously, and it's contagious. Take some time to encounter the wisdom of this incredible person, and you, too, will grow more generous."

– **Stephan Tchividjian**, CEO & Founder, National Christian Foundation, South Florida

"The world is lucky that they will receive what we received as Elizabeth's clients for over twenty years—Christian and inspiring financial insights and encouragement."

– **Darrell Gwynn**, NHRA Hall of Fame drag racer, Top 50 Drivers of all Time

"Elizabeth Brickman has been a trusted VOICE in the Christian Community on finances for decades. This book is going to have an impact on people my age and for many generations to come."

– **Dr. Bob Barnes**, CEO, Sheridan House Family Ministries, Co-Host, Parenting on Purpose Podcast, and Author

"Spend any time with Elizabeth Brickman, and you will walk away inspired and empowered. God has entrusted rich insight to her, which saturates her coaching, podcasts and writings. Those who share a faith community with Elizabeth know why this winsome wisdom is so effortlessly dispensed. It flows from a deep reservoir of faith in God's timeless truths."

– **Dr. Robey Barnes**, Lead Pastor, City Rev Church

End Game Press books may be purchased in bulk at special discounts for sales promotion, corporate gifts, ministry, fund-raising, or educational purposes. Special editions can also be created to specifications. For details, contact Special Sales Dept., End Game Press, P.O. Box 206, Nesbit, MS 38651 or info@endgamepress.com. Visit our website at www.endgamepress.com.

Library of Congress Control Number: 2024951492
ISBN: 978-1-63797-252-6
eBook ISBN: 978-1-63797-253-3

Cover design by: Dan Pitts
Interior by Monica Thomas for TLC Book Design, *TLCBookDesign.com*

Printed in the United States of America
10 9 8 7 6 5 4 3 2 1

I dedicate this book to my
beloved former clients.

Thank you for teaching and inspiring me.
May the impact of your lessons and example
be magnified, and may God be glorified.
To know you is to love you—and
through all these years, I do.

Blessed is the person who does not
walk in the counsel of the wicked,
Nor stand in the path of sinners,
Nor sit in the seat of scoffers!
But his delight is in the Law of the LORD,
And on His Law he meditates day and night.
He will be like a tree planted by streams of water,
Which yields its fruit in its season,
And its leaf does not wither;
And in whatever he does, he prospers.

PSALM 1:1-3 NASB

TABLE *of* CONTENTS

Part I

Your Financial Awakening

CLOSE THE GAPS

Chapter One

WHY MY STORY MIGHT SAVE YOUR FINANCIAL FUTURE

I was born to parents of wealth. But their wealth was not blessed.

First, we lost our housekeeper. Then, we lost our house. First, we were rich. Then, we were poor.

By age ten, I knew all too well how both sides lived.

Young children don't perceive poverty or wealth. They're enriched and comforted by the familiar. I was too young at the time to grasp the meaning of "financial implosion." I knew only that I'd lost my house, my neighborhood, my school, and all my friends.

My parents were good people—disciplined, dedicated, and driven. Objectively, they were among the smartest entrepreneurial individuals I've ever known, with IQs likely at genius level.

But their financial strategy missed a few key pieces of God's great financial puzzle, and unfortunately, those tiny missing pieces were enough to push them onto an avoidable track of ruin.

I know what it is to suffer a financial fall from grace and to experience a life-changing freefall into overwhelming loss.

But I also know what it is to recover—to reconstruct a life of sustaining financial elegance throughout varying financial seasons, artfully manage the subtleties of risk, and enjoy contentment—the kind of financial contentment that precedes wealth.

We don't need to know finance—just God's finance laws. Because what you don't know can impoverish you, or break your heart, or both. Those who think they can navigate our unmanageable world without inviting God's active involvement into every sphere, especially finances, are mistaken. The Bible is loaded with over two thousand instructions on how to earn, grow, save, spend, and interact with wealth. How can we afford to miss this timeless financial instruction?

God redeemed my family's financial trauma and weaved His greater good into our lives. My dear parents started over, and each went on to become highly successful business owners who lived financially and emotionally rewarding lives. A third beloved parent and five much-loved siblings were later added to our family. God made whole what had been broken.

By His amazing grace, I was given a chance to receive back from God all that the locusts had eaten. It wasn't easy, and it wasn't fast. But through business enterprise, I learned about money, both professionally *and* personally.

As is His redemptive nature, the Lord led me into a rewarding career as a financial advisor and investment professional. What a privilege to help clients escape financial heartache and despair. For twenty-five years, I vowed to block impoverishment from sabotaging any client under my watch. If poverty wanted to take them down, it would have to get past me. Not that I had any special powers to protect them. But I'd made a serious study of biblical finance.

I knew the rules of the game—*His* game.

It was a deeply satisfying mission.

My clients were dear, highly accomplished men and women who'd worked hard to earn, save, and invest. Yet, as remarkable and successful as they were, I was surprised at how very many struggled with anxiety, heartache, and distress.

The wealthy are often a misunderstood—and emotionally underserved—demographic.

It may be hard to appreciate, but when people work their hearts out to achieve wealth because they believe it will insulate them from life's sorrows, and after reaching their goals are met with impossible life disappointments that wealth can't fix, it can be emotionally devastating. Just like the rest of us, the wealthy need comfort, counsel, and compassion.

I considered the discipline, hard work, innovation, value-creation, and perseverance that grew and fertilized wealth. And I felt increasing respect for the grit and determination that contributed to my clients becoming society's givers instead of takers. Yet, I saw little attention was paid to the emotional needs of these diligent and industrious people who worked hard, sacrificed, and eventually did well.

As a demographic, the wealthy are the least understood or supported financial category. Their imperfect choices do not necessarily stem from an obsession with wealth, as they are so often accused. Their choices and actions are usually just a survival cry for relief from anxiety, pain, fear, and isolation—yes, isolation. The wealthy do not feel safe discussing private financial matters with others, and many times bear life's deepest conflicts and questions alone.

No wonder some turn to unfortunate financial behavior for relief. This book aims to fix that.

My wealthy clients had financial freedom, but it did not free them from suffering. For some, unhealed childhood experiences had damaged their relationship with money. Anxiety-riddled others feared they might make a mistake or miss an opportunity. Some worried the market would disappoint. Or worse, they'd be the ones to disappoint...their families, friends, and, most dreaded, their peers.

Maybe you share some of these same struggles.

Oh, the price of unblessed wealth! How miserable are those who have wealth without financial happiness. Underneath the trappings of riches are the poorest humans in the world. I know these people. They are wonderful. And they are real.

You may not know anyone like that, but I've known many. These dear people are more restless and desperate than most because they've already earned what they thought would fill the inner void, *but it did not.* Money without purpose is a sad state of being. Is it any wonder we hear about billionaires on cocaine? Millionaires who commit suicide?

Money is a wonderful tool. But money does not have the power to save. We need a Savior for that.

I've witnessed rampant financial unhappiness among those of every economic status, including the wealthy. Many tears of heartache have been shed at my desk. I've grieved with beautiful clients who live wealthy, yet heartbroken lives. Some of my most cherished clients were rich on the outside, yet impoverished on the inside—living in outward luxury but spiritual bankruptcy.

But it doesn't have to be that way. Wealth can be positive and purpose-driven, propelling ever higher levels of faith and joy.

I'm ready to stand with you against unseen financial forces that oppose you.

- The memories and hurts of your past.
- The undue influence of the unwise in your life.
- The frustration of being misunderstood by just about everybody.
- The disdain of someone with less money who resents you for having rightly earned and carefully managed yours.
- The psychological tricks of unscrupulous marketers who use your hidden heartache and needs against you.
- And the resistance sent from hell itself.

Yes—financial opposition surrounds you. And some may be buried within you.

Traditional investment strategies cannot solve the issues and unhappiness that plague the wealthy. These numerically based strategies approach finance as if separate and distinct from our human needs for love, purpose, acceptance, and significance. They try to bypass profound truths about the source of money, the purpose of money, and the blessing—or curse—that wealth can be in our lives.

Wealth can be a blessing; I want you to have it. But if wealth is not blessed, it will not satisfy—and it will not last. Wealth without God's financial wisdom at the very center is a terrible trap.

What Does It Mean to Be Wealth-Blessed?

For twenty-five years, I witnessed up close the winning ways and spiritual disciplines that propel certain special individuals toward ever-higher states of financial happiness and significance. I'm going to take you behind the scenes of real former clients who are living well and serving God. Enjoying the fruit of God's Kingdom while using money as a tool to serve Him—and Him alone. We'll explore the emotions, attitudes, and beliefs that set them on a higher footing.

Come with me as we strengthen your life of godly financial elegance. Let's close the gaps, heal the hurts, and put God at the center.

Invite God into Your Wealth Story

God has provided a foundation, a structure, from which you and I can make wise and elegant financial decisions for personal and Kingdom impact. You can avoid the perils of bad decisions, be spared unnecessary heartache, and enjoy a happy and holy relationship with money.

To be clear, the affluence I endorse is *not* the false and dangerous theology of the so-called "prosperity gospel." God owns everything. We own nothing. Once we grasp this life-transforming truth—that all the world's assets belong to Him and none to us—we open ourselves to receive and manage true wealth that can be blessed with no sorrow added to it.

Affluence, money flowing through us, is not for our sake. It's for the Kingdom's sake. Through us. For Him. This is the vibrant pulse of the wealth-blessed.

That's why this book is not about stocks, bonds, or investments. Excellent advisors are everywhere to help you manage your portfolio. My mission is to support you with an elegant financial lifestyle as a person of faith. To help you experience joy and deep significance in the wealth God allows to flow through your hands.

Living a spiritually elegant lifestyle means we do things His way, not ours. To help us succeed, He's painstakingly written explicit financial instructions on ancient transcripts. You can create a financial life that will satisfy you and glorify God.

Attaching His principles to your portfolio won't bind or constrain you. It will free and invigorate you. It will sharply focus you on the meaningful financial life He intends for you, which is far better than any financial life you could design for yourself.

The wealth-blessed are private, quiet, and humble. They don't reveal their intimate processes to most, but for twenty-five years, they entrusted them to me. With an insider's advantage, and without breaching confidentiality, I'll share with you how these individuals work, play, think, and live, and how they process their pain, fear, and longings.

Watch them. You'll be inspired. They are a crystal-clear vision of who you can be and how you can live.

We'll undertake a search-and-destroy mission to uncover unhealed financial wounds currently blocking your own wealth-blessed future. Together, we'll expose and clean out old hurts causing financial unhappiness or dysfunction.

I'm not a therapist, but God is. He will perform His financial therapy. And I will hold your hand.

May the healing process begin. You'll understand your financial self in a way you never did before. The past informs the future, but will no longer control it. For God has His purpose in the wealth that flows through you, His beloved, however large or little that flow may presently be.

It's never too late to step into the fullness of His plan. Now is your time to receive all God has ordained for you to have, to be, and to do. Through Him, you possess untapped power to direct the course of your financial affairs, improve your present happiness, build a lifestyle of financial elegance, and make a significant Kingdom impact.

I've watched countless clients rise above, and stay above, their former circumstances.

I am one of them. Generational curses are broken. Finances fall into line.

You can recalibrate the anxious present, heal from your financial past, and learn to manage wealth with finesse. When the unexpected comes, you'll feel strong and capable—not panicked. In every financial season, you'll walk confidently along your wealth-blessed path.

Calm in the storm. Capable in strategy. Satisfied in the present.

What a wondrous way to live!

I hope you'll embrace the easy but essential biblical principles of this book. These are *jewels* that will save you much financial despair.

You need no longer live frustrated, fearful, or wanting.

Begin this very day.

Chapter Two

WHY DO SMART PEOPLE MAKE POOR FINANCIAL DECISIONS?

Many of us have a secret love-hate relationship with money, *and we should.*

- If the money intended to fix us becomes the very thing that exposes the worst in us…
- If the money intended to heal our past becomes a billboard advertising our shame…
- If the money intended to strengthen our relationships becomes the issue that spoils them…
- If the money intended to answer our prayers becomes the tempter of our sins…

You can see why love-hate may be a defining relationship with our money.

This need not be. Our goal is emotional wholeness and spiritual wellness around money that allows us to enjoy a sin-free, purpose-driven relationship with finances and be wealth-blessed by God. We can have this. God wants us to have it.

The only path to financial happiness is if our inner wellness is stronger than our outer wealth. Neither love nor hate has any place in our relationship with money.

If that's not how life is for you presently, we can fix it, and we must.

If our relationship with money is dysfunctional, no additional money will ever repair it. More money will only create more opportunities for dysfunction. It's love-hate on a grander scale. If our relationship with money is toxic, no amount of money will cleanse it. The news reports tragic suicides of those who had all the wealth one could hope for but none of the peace needed to survive.

Even mild levels of financial dysfunction and unhappiness can have a destabilizing effect on our lives. We see it in others…

In a loved one or a close friend whose actions swing from impulse to regret.

Whose left and right financial turns are unpredictable and unplanned.

Whose financial situation is exhausting to watch and even more exhausting to live.

Who may even be wealthy, but surely aren't living blessed.

Who may be brilliant, but whose financial mindset is damaged, leading to foolish choices.

Who may be believers, but God is absent from their finances.

A toxic relationship with money is a financial relationship we would not choose and would never want, but there it may be, ready to torment us. We cannot escape, divorce, or move away from interacting with money. For better or for worse, for richer or for poorer, we will be tethered to a relationship with money all the days of our lives…so let's take charge and make it the best relationship it can be.

Since our relationship with money functions like a compass, steering our every money decision, the question is well worth asking…Where is your financial compass taking you?

Is anything from your past interfering with your ability to live an elegant, wealth-blessed life? Consider for a moment what money means to you.

Is it your nemesis? Your foe?

Your love? Your surrogate parent?

Your god?

Sometimes, we repel wealth for subversive reasons. A secret hurt may be buried inside our consciousness, hiding under deep cover of memory and past suffering. That pain or shame distorts into baseless lies that drive us toward a persistent, unwanted result. Maybe there's a hidden payoff for our constant financial angst.

Then they'll love me. Then they'll notice me.

Then they'll feel sorry for me. Then they'll realize I'm suffering. Then they'll see how deeply they damaged me.

Then they'll know they should have done a better job. Then they'll rescue me. Then I won't have to try—and risk failing.

Then I won't expose that I'm not good enough. Then they'll see how wrong they were.

Confront the Lies

But you see, every one of these thoughts is a damaging lie trespassing in your head. There will be no reckoning "then." By God's grace, design, and holy purpose, He's given us now. It is you who will determine your financial path ahead. Not "they"—not the hurtful people from your past, but you. I think of these disempowering thoughts as lying financial criminals. Don't give them shelter. Expose them and destroy them, so you can experience God's financial wholeness from the inside out.

Why accept a toxic relationship with money without resistance?

Toxins, once identified, are usually removed from our homes and our lives. But no matter how toxic our relationship is with money, we cannot survive without it.

You'll have to remain in intimate and highly active engagement with money all the days of your life.

Until you redefine the dynamics of that relationship, the *nature* of that relationship; until you insist, in uncompromising fashion, on God's sovereign rulership over that relationship, you might sabotage your own financial future.

To Move Forward, Let's Briefly Go Back

Why examine our emotional wounds? Simple. To keep ourselves from repelling wealth.

Our past, with all its hurts, sins, and memories, shapes our relationship with money, propelling us toward financial wholeness or holding us back into brokenness, unhappiness, or angst.

It's possible that the financial unrest you feel is caused by the lingering presence of unhealed wounds or unhealthy patterns of thinking. We are the carriers of God's wealth. But hurting hands cannot carry wealth well at all. Our inner damage seeps out through our relationship with money.

Until you master your relationship with money, any financial strategy you devise will be inherently flawed. In fact, you might be adding avoidable financial risk to your life.

Let's firm up our financial identity and shake off anything that would stop the flow of God's money for God's purposes. Let us lay aside the weight of the past and break free. Let's ask the Lord, standing firmly in the truth of His Word, to resolve our identity and conflict.

Financial wholeness is well worth seeking, not just for yourself, but also for the beloved others in your life. It will impact generations to come.

Let's figure out everything preventing you from reaching your highest ordained wealth. For if you were to gain wealth in an unhealed state, it would only destroy you—and ultimately destroy itself.

What Trips You Up?

Our damaged relationship with money may partly be due to unhealed wounds. We are all wounded. Each wound closes differently. And sometimes, they don't close at all.

We may think we're well and financially whole until something unexpected happens that undermines our confidence and footing. Unhealed wounds linger, dormant, ready to awaken without warning whenever a current event evokes a painful memory from our past.

At those times, wounds pop up like a menacing jack-in-the-box in a horror film. Our senses flood with a sudden, intense need to survive.

How We Accidentally Create Financial Sabotage

Money talks. It reveals the framework behind our thinking when we cannot find our words. The way we interact with money demonstrates so much about our unhealed state. A spending pattern is an excellent diagnostic tool. It pinpoints the wounded places in our hearts and minds where we're *desperately seeking to be heard or understood...*

If I suffer emotional hurt and use money to relieve my hurt, I pay a steep price: it costs me continuing unhappiness and, ultimately, any chance at growing godly wealth.

The only way to shake off a destructive financial pattern is to expose the underlying feelings behind it. Feelings are subversive. They infiltrate the way we relate to money. They show up as habits but act out like curses, which can become generational. If we don't take control, we pass our unfortunate patterns down to the next generation. Our children and grandchildren will either emulate our damaged relationship with money or react with an opposite dysfunction.

We don't have to follow the financial paths of generations before us.

The primary mission of money is to sustain life and glorify God through Kingdom generosity to His beloveds. But in our unhealed woundedness, we may use money to accomplish a very different purpose...

To Punish

To punish someone for not having provided for us.

To punish ourselves for a past sin we believe is unforgivable.

To Parent

To parent ourselves because our parents did not. We indulge any delight we fancy as a mock-imitation of the parental love we continue to seek well into adulthood.

If a formerly indulgent parent is deceased, we may attempt to replicate what parental love felt like to us as a child. Or we may try to gratify ourselves the same way a doting parent did so we can recreate the carefree way we felt under our parents' benevolent care.

To Please

We fear we cannot please a certain person without money. We want them to like us, include us, approve us, and accept us. We try to please them by saying yes without boundaries or limits to any expense they wish us to incur. We never question. We're overly generous with gifts—only because they expect it.

To Protect

To overprotect a healthy, able-bodied adult who doesn't need our protection.

Our hyper-protection exposes our lack of faith in God's sovereign oversight. Sometimes, the one under our overprotection would be far better served to go out into the world and be forced to discover—and monetize—the wonderful gifts God has planted inside them.

To Play

We're overworked and overwrought. Too exhausted for healthier forms of play, we become vulnerable to advertisers flooding us with the fantasy of a different life, which they promise can be our life, too, if we purchase their expensive product. See the happy, smiling, carefree people around the car/boat/fill-in-the-blank? Aren't they proof our fatigue will disappear, our social lives will improve, and our spouse and kids will get along?

Maybe you work hard, yet are uncelebrated by others. Or resent others for not making possible the fun and refreshment you crave.

To Perform

To wear money like a costume, presenting an illusion of something we want others to believe about us. We want to be noticed, show off, or stand out to a certain audience we wish to win over. Perhaps we've felt unnoticed or underappreciated in the past. Now, we want to show others we have wealth and, therefore, deserve admiration, status, and respect.

To Pacify

To pacify a hurting, sad, or depressed self—or another. Perhaps we couldn't calm an out-of-control parent. Our only way to feel safe was to keep them pacified. We may carry that survival instinct into adulthood and reenact it using money again and again.

To Prove

To spend money we don't have because we have an urgent something to prove—in quiet, angry, payback style. We may "prove," by our spending decisions, that our high school yearbook was wrong when they said we were most likely NOT to succeed. We may "prove" we didn't deserve a terrible thing that was said about us or done to us.

Our insistence to prove is often triggered by an insatiable need to right a wrong. We throw endless funds against our injustice. And then we learn, after consuming all we have, that some wrongs can never be righted by spending money.

To Possess Power

To possess power so that "our will be done"—and no other. To make our voice important enough to be heard. To possess unquestionable authority. Sometimes, a docile child who was beaten or bullied grows up to be a power-hungry adult who uses money to avoid getting hurt.

To Pretend

We pretend to have wealth we do not have to feel good about ourselves because we believe our true self is lacking and insufficient. Though the world deems us a success, in our secret place, we feel like worthless imposters. We use money as a pretense to add to the illusion that we are special—because we don't believe it.

To Pursue

To pursue someone whose heart we desire to win. This might be a prospective mate we believe would not love us for being who we are, or a social group we want to be part of, one whose lifestyle may be far costlier than ours. Or we may use money to pursue a course of action we believe would otherwise be denied us by God.

Rules of Engagement

A damaged relationship with money would gladly rule our subconscious—and maybe ruin our lives. In the coming chapters, we'll ask the Lord to kiss our boo-boos to make them better and to bind our deeper wounds as only He can.

God will do His Financial Therapy. And I will hold your hand.

No matter your financial history, God does not want you to allow your past to wreck your financial future. Establish your rules of engagement, namely, with you as master, and money as servant. That's the only relationship you want.

Know your financial triggers. Stay financially alert. Never spend wealth from dysfunction. Spend as a deliberate act of worship, praise, and trust.

In future chapters, we'll explore how wealth-blessed people joyfully earn *and* spend for the *glory of God*. Self-awareness will help you choose from a higher plane than your old, damaged auto-response system. Spiritual awareness will keep you safe from being triggered at all.

Managing money is like herding puppies—the puppies want to go everywhere. But do not worry. Money is impossible to train, but not impossible to lead.

And lead you will, with a sure-footed, elegant biblical approach. Money will soon walk beside you like an obedient puppy without a leash. It will sit when you say sit. It will stay when you say stay.

Chapter Three

WHY PEOPLE STRUGGLE WITH THE CONFLICTS OF WEALTH

Is wealth sinful? Is poverty holy? Dare I seek more?

Admit it, as Christians, we're conflicted about money and success. We don't want the tiresome subject of money to be the sun of our days or the moon of our sleepless nights.

At the same time, we see the advantages of wealth in the hands of God's people. In a community crisis, we'd rather be the one equipped to act than the one standing on the sidelines.

In an emergency, we long to respond with, *I will,* instead of *I wish I could.*

Inwardly, we wrestle with social and moral issues. At times, the disparity between those who have and have not seems random and unjust. Having more than we need, we grieve for the loved one—or the stranger—who never seems to have enough.

Is Money Evil?

Many good people believe money is evil. I respectfully disagree.

If money were evil, why would a loving God offer so much detailed biblical instruction on how to earn it, grow it, spend it, give it, invest it, and bequeath it when we die? If God were against money, why would He fill Scripture with 2,300 explicit instructions on how to manage it?

Scripture is positively loaded with ways to attain money—along with numerous warnings and instructions about its use and dangers. These warnings are not contradictions. Money is a big subject. The Bible contains more references to money than to heaven and hell—combined.

God, who is the sole owner of all the money in the world, continuously appoints ordinary people like you and me to manage large sums, sometimes exceedingly large sums, to fulfill His purposes.

You may think money is evil and that God hates money, but He doesn't. God hates idolatry. He hates it when we fall in love with an asset that belongs to Him alone. The root of financial evil is only in the arrogant *love* of money—not in its godly stewardship.

What a high and noble honor to live responsibly rich, entrusted by God to deliver His wealth to His beloveds, empowered to give more generously than you ever dreamed.

Is wealth evil? Not in the hands of those who use wealth to glorify God.

But sometimes wealth is cursed

- ...if it is acquired deceitfully.
- ...if it fools you into believing your wealth belongs to you and not to God.
- ...if it causes you to sin.
- ...if it becomes your god.
- ...if it causes you to imagine YOU are God.

Is It Holy to Hate Money?

Since money is rife with spiritual risks, some well-meaning people of faith insist the only alternative to sin is to disdain it. Disdain *feels* like a holy attitude. But is it?

I'm curious about those who disdain money. If we surrender all wealth to unbelievers, who will support our churches and ministries? Who will fund Kingdom causes?

Suppose all Christians become society's receivers instead of givers. The body of Christ will have no choice but to turn to secular sources, such as the government, for provision. But governments do not, by law, provide grants or funding for Christian churches and ministries. Without funding, small churches and ministries would be forced to close.

If godly people commit themselves to being poor, in which direction will society's balance of wealth tilt? You know the answer: Toward the secular hands of those whose purposes oppose God. All the wealth in the land will soon be handed off to individuals who, let's be frank, hate God.

Having surrendered our personal opportunity to earn wealth, will these unbelievers, in our place, promote the gospel for us? No, they will not. Those who do not love the Lord are unlikely to support Kingdom causes.

That's why we cannot let the Lord's ministries go unfunded. This responsibility belongs to us. We must never surrender financial control to people who don't love God.

God's beloved must become strong earners, investors, and givers with the financial means—and the firm mindset—to fund Kingdom causes. We, the strong in Christ, must rise up and financially support the cause of Christ. This is wealth's highest purpose.

Can Ambition Be Holy?

We dream big dreams, don't we? Yours may be to build or expand a business or create a large legacy. You may yearn to make an extraordinary financial impact in a particular way.

As a Christian with a mindset surrendered to Christ, do you ever wonder if it's right to dream at all? Perhaps you feel magnetized, drawn to a certain occupation for no explainable reason. You feel "called" to a particular business or career path and wonder if God could be behind it.

Isn't it amazing to consider that your dream may be His dream for you?

"For we are His workmanship, created in Christ Jesus for good works, which God prepared beforehand that we should walk in them" (Ephesians 2:10, NASB).

In accordance with His brilliant plan to seek and save the lost, the Lord may have inspired you with a passion to do something…be something…or accomplish something. This is the Great Strategist at work, guiding your life plan.

You fret it was your human ego that thought up the grand idea. You rightly bring your passion to the altar. And you do not seek wealth for its own sake. The exaggerated claims of the prosperity gospel do not fool you. You want His true path, the narrow road that leads to life.

Yet some dreams were born in God's own heart, and not your own, imperceptibly planted by the Father Himself to orchestrate His grand plan via your anointed life. He gives intuition to the heart and instinct to the mind (see Job 38:36). Humbling, I know.

Since it is His will to seek and save the lost, the Lord may have stirred within you a dream to occupy a particular space where the lost reside. This need not surprise you. His tactical plan is to send His believing children (us) to the C-suites, executive offices, golf courses, courtrooms, classrooms, and other places where His beloved work and play and live—which, for the most part, is not in church.

Serving the Lord with all your heart, soul, mind, and strength doesn't confine you to official ministry. Your talent and drive may reflect God's call to minister in ways unimagined, following creative paths He's prepared just for you.

As ambassadors for Christ, we are torch carriers into every dark space. Imagine the good you can do in almost any endeavor. At this moment, somewhere far away, a parent is praying for their child, over whom you—yes, you—will have professional or societal influence.

Whatever your calling, you will "*be* church and *bring* church" to many lives. Because our lives are ordained, all our days are in ministry—the hardworking days, the business-building days, and yes, even the vacation days.

Can a Vacation Be Holy?

My husband had meticulously arranged our dream vacation. Fifty pounds of photography equipment stood packed and ready for takeoff. His plan was for the two of us to take a private African photo safari and experience the beauty of wildlife in its unspoiled natural habitat.

My plan was to relax, photograph a lion or two, and enjoy a much-needed vacation. I did not plan to "*be* church or *bring* church" to anyone for sixteen blessed days.

Then our flight was rerouted.

Looking back, I realize our entire trip was ordained, right down to the plane's emergency landing and missed connections. Through an amazing set of circumstances, I had the unexpected privilege of comforting someone with the love of Christ and offering her a path out of darkness into light. Later that week, I stood beside her in an empty tour bus, trembling in awe as she was baptized with a half-filled bottle of water. I learned that her mother, who lived in a distant country, far away, had prayed for many years for her daughter to come to faith.

I planned only to take a vacation. God planned to save a life. In His hands, even a dream vacation can be made holy.

Whose Mission Is It, Anyway?

Each of us has been assigned a glorious mission to radiate the very fragrance of Christ into every corner of the earth and to persons at every level of society—at the very top and the very bottom. That means we bring Christ into the boardroom, stateroom, and stockroom, too. Part of His divine plan is to embed us in a specific sphere of influence. You were born for a purpose. Make no mistake: He made you to be there.

Are you a chief executive officer, investment banker, or multinational entrepreneur? God wants His loved ones to spread out, with impact, throughout the earth. So, you no longer need to fear accomplishment, wealth, or success. It is He who gives us the ability to earn wealth—for His purposes (see Deuteronomy 8:18).

Everything you have can be used for His Kingdom. Everything you do can be used to glorify Him.

So, pay close attention to every door and opportunity He opens for you. The favor you receive is not accidental. God equips you to be productive for His sake. We have come into this world divinely pre-wired with talents and innate abilities to do powerful good in His name.

Our job is to will and to do of His good pleasure. How compassionate that He plants big dreams into our hearts, so it won't be too hard for us to reach high to attain them.

Though a dream burning in your heart may not involve the church or ministry, there is still cause for holy excitement. The ministries embedded in the world of business are thrilling, rewarding, and fun. As a person of influence working as God's appointed agent in your successful career, you have privileged access to woo God's beloved to the unconditional, unabashed love of Christ.

- As a physician, you might diagnose a broken spirit.
- As a financier, you may lead your clients to true wealth.
- As an executive administrator, you may administer prayer.
- As a real estate broker, you may help a family come home to faith.

Everywhere you look, you find God's beloveds. God is calling you. Your clients and customers, your partners and patients, are waiting for you.

They will not be found at church. They're at brokerages and banks, galas and galleries, hotels and hospitals. The church must come to them on their terms—to their environment, their hospital room, and maybe to their home. You and I can be the church.

One famous South Florida tycoon was brought to faith by a humble housepainter in his backyard. Thank God for that housepainter.

The church is you. That's why you'll do well to seek almost any enterprise that excites and electrifies you. Your innate abilities are on purpose, for His purpose.

On her sixtieth birthday, one of my attorney friends dreamed of raising a million dollars for local Christian ministries by forming a women's giving circle. She imagined each member would donate $1,000 annually, and all funds would be given to well-vetted ministries.

Before her seventieth birthday, one million dollars had been given away.

This is where money starts to excite me:

- When we replace divisive inner conflict with highly focused wealth purpose.
- When we replace despair over the fruitlessness of wealth with holy intention.
- When we replace disdain with joyful stewardship.
- When we replace dread of loss with a passion for giving.
- When we replace duty with honor and excitement—especially the excitement of generosity.

Focus your central navigation system on Him, and you can pursue big dreams without losing your way.

You can live extraordinarily well without abandoning your faith by finding the courage to manage your big life for the glory of God.

If you step into the fullness of who He made you to be, inviting God to write your wealth story, and embracing, without fear, a mission-driven life of dreams you confidently and actively pursue, He'll place you in a sphere where you'll shine as a radiant instrument of His love (Philippians 2:15). You'll experience the humbling joy of holy impact. And one day, someone's parent, in a distant country, far away, may thank God for sending you (2 Corinthians 9:12-14).

Chapter Four

WHY WE NEED A WEALTH MAP

On what financial ground do you stand now? Does your wealth feel blessed? Or cursed? Do you feel...financially secure? Anxious? Or in distress?

Are You Financially Secure?

If you're financially secure, your income and assets reflect God's provision, so relax. You need not grasp tightly, nor be anxious about your next mission. God owns all the wealth in the land and has already chosen to assign some to your care and stewardship. Without His permission, no amount of talent or hard work on your part will result in profit. Scripture says it this way: *"You may say to yourself, 'My power and the strength of my hands have produced this wealth for me.' But remember the LORD your God, for it is he who gives you the ability to produce wealth...."* (Deuteronomy 8:17-18a).

You've worked hard. You've made good decisions. You were diligent when others slacked—well done, my friend. And it is God who gave you the ability and opportunity to produce wealth.

God is no accidental player in your wealth story. He is its architect.

Your Path

Love the LORD, not the money. Follow His, and only His, financial principles.

Rely only on Him, not on your financial statement. Demonstrate extreme generosity because you are not an owner, but a highly trusted, well-rewarded manager of all He ordains to pass through your hands.

Keep yourself from being polluted by the world.

Your Posture

Hands wide open, not grasping. Eyes on Him. Ears inclined to the whisper of the Holy Spirit, not the blare of godless advertisers seeking to empty your wealth via products that never satisfy.

Your Prayer

Here I am, Lord, Your trusted servant. You are the Author and Hero of my wealth story. Please bless my mission and purpose. How much wealth may I distribute for Your purposes over my lifetime? One hundred thousand dollars? One million? Ten times more?

Are You Financially Anxious?

There isn't enough, you worry. Or is there? You're just not sure.

You trust the Lord. Your advisors assure you that you are sound and solvent. But you feel shadowed by a profound financial anxiety you cannot shake.

On financially sunny days, of which you have plenty, you tell yourself you're faring well. Then, a storm rolls in via an unplanned expense, and your financial sunlight dims.

You don't mean to be double-minded, and your concerns are justifiable. But anxiety is a tender mindset. Pay close attention.

Fear clouds judgment, and can lead to error, especially if you keep switching financial strategies in a frantic, zigzag attempt to get it right. And what if the basis for your anxiety is not even true?

Don't stuff feelings of financial anxiety. Left unchallenged, they'll hound, distract, and weaken you.

Confront these feelings head-on. Ask the Lord to help you understand their roots—and what He might have you do about them. He may be offering you an opportunity to examine the wobbly underpinnings of your business or lifestyle. The Holy Spirit may be stirring you to adjust a flawed financial perception or plan, or a falsehood driving your concerns.

Admittedly, there is much uncertainty in this temporary land we call home, a land rampant with heresies like the prosperity gospel. False teaching makes us vulnerable to subtle shifts in attitude, philosophy, or behavior. Ask God what He would have you do about your uncertainty. Don't miss a wonderful chance to receive His divine financial guidance.

We are not of the world, but we're living in the thick of its brush for now. Financial uncertainty surrounds you—but must never be granted dominion *over* you. You belong to the Lord. What feels uncertain to you is by no means uncertain to Him.

He may be seeking your full attention to strengthen, prepare, and equip you to take on a larger financial responsibility than you've ever known. Now may be His appointed time to finesse your stewardship anew for a holy and significant purpose. Today's uncertainty may later prove to be the greatest thing that ever happened to you—if you bring your uncertainty to Him.

Don't linger another moment in financial quicksand. Pray with an open heart for God to reveal what's missing in your financial affairs, and what you can do about it. If you discover any weakness holding you back from your fullest potential, release it to the One who can help you overcome it.

We are given this one and only life, filled with uncertainty and challenges, and it's passing quickly.

A fresh perspective may be in order. I promise this is for your benefit—not about self-condemnation, but a bold new conviction to manage God's money God's way, as you reach and stretch for the fullest satisfaction of His ordained provision.

Invite God into your wealth story. Establish a biblically firm financial footing at the outset. Meet with your advisors again to confirm whether you have a genuine basis for economic insecurity and learn precisely what you can do about it. Take immediate action to shore up your foundation.

Uncertainty is a pervasive fog that hovers over the earth and its inhabitants.

Yet, there are three things about which you may be very certain: your path, your place, and your God.

Certain of Your Path

If you listen for His voice over the din, the Lord will lead you. Exercise dogged persistence in managing money His way, not yours. Be active, not passive, in living with financial and spiritual wellness. Even in the midst of inevitable challenges and adversities that arise along the way, learn to appreciate the subtle intricacies of your progress:

Measure gain in courage, skill, outlook, and outreach.

Measure profit spiritually as well as financially.

God stands at the center of your future. You can be certain of your path.

Certain of Your Place

It's time to free yourself from residual insecurity about your social, professional, or societal status. Shed the weighty scales of needing to prove your value via human position or man-made possessions. Whether your next mission succeeds or if God uses it to redirect you to something else, your life is ordained, and your position in Christ is secure. You can be certain of your place in the Kingdom and this world.

Certain of Your God

God loves you. He paid the ultimate price to save you. Despite your financial uncertainty, His ultimate plan is always for your good. He wants no weapon formed against you to prosper. Turn to Him as your unceasing source of wisdom, direction, instruction, correction, and provision. You can well-afford to trust and serve Him wholeheartedly. You can be certain of your God.

Your Path

Invite God into your wealth story. Actively participate in a biblical financial lifestyle.

Seek the counsel of godly financial advisors to show you the realities of your assets. Insist your financial plan adheres to God's directions—especially His plan for giving.

Reduce or eliminate any expenditures that do not align with your spiritual values. Be watchful of the financial whirlwind around you, asking the Lord if its source is from heaven.

Enjoy these precious, ordained days of your life. Pursue your mission without fear. God may have big plans ahead for you.

Begin to practice radical generosity. Show Him what you will do with much—by doing much with little.

Your Posture

Shoulders erect and attentive. Muscles at the ready. Eyes closed to envy.

Ears closed to unbiblical wealth-gaining strategies and get-rich-quick schemes. Mouth closed to grumbling.

Feet shod with the readiness to work, save, invest, spend, and give according to His good pleasure. Tireless in faith and trust. Mind alert to cast down imaginations, take thoughts captive, and refocus on God's Word.

Your Prayer

Father, You know my coming and my going. Search me, O God, and know my heart. Test my anxious thoughts. Please bless my mission—or show me Yours. Point out anything You find in me that makes You sad and lead me on the everlasting way.

Are You Financially Distressed?

Are you trapped in a slow-motion financial freefall? Is the wealth you worked so hard to build imploding before your eyes? Are you straining to hold back a financial tsunami from swallowing your assets and your life? There's no need to accept today's struggle as if it's tomorrow's destiny. It doesn't have to be.

Jesus said the poor will always be with us, but He didn't call out the poor by name. Why embrace a soon-to-be-poor identity unless He explicitly assigns it?

Or have you already lost everything? Are you starting over? Being poor doesn't have to be the end of your wealth story. Why, perhaps you're only in training.

Maybe you were born to *feed* the poor.

A circumstance beyond your control may have ushered you into a season of poverty. But you can extract incredible lessons from this temporary season.

The Lord may be calling you to develop highly advanced and disciplined financial skills to prepare for a different life than the life you lived before and are struggling to survive. You may be in excruciating training only to receive His divine appointment to deliver vast stores of Kingdom wealth into Kingdom hands.

Remain calm. Dig out in confident perseverance, His way, not your way—and maybe not what some experts tell you is the obvious way. Follow His road and no other. No shortcuts for you unless they align with His Word.

Your Path

Build financial muscles now—even before you crystallize a vision for rebuilding your future. No matter how advanced your financial mastery, earnestly learn about money from God's perspective and no other. Commit to doing everything within your power to grow spiritually and financially as strong as He allows.

Forget your master's degree in finance for just a moment or two. Develop biblical financial expertise instead. True financial wisdom—the kind that can change your circumstances and life—is found in the Word of God.

Seek godly counsel. No matter how desperate your circumstance, don't be led astray by any strategy that doesn't adhere to biblical guidelines. Be wary and alert. Whatever occurs around you, continually ask Him if its source is from Heaven.

Grow daily into a financially fit vessel, ready to receive and release the unblocked flow of His resources. You don't have to be perfect—only prepared.

Give generously to Kingdom causes from the "firstfruits" of your earnings. Don't wait until you're financially whole again to resume giving. Start now as a deliberate, disciplined act of worship, praise, and trust.

Your Posture

Head bowed in humility; hands extended heavenward in faith. Eyes on Him in watchful trust.

Ears shut to whispers of doubt. Tongue repeating God's promises. Disposition calm because you trust.

Your Prayer

Father, I'd be swallowed up by financial catastrophe were it not for Your mercy. I surrender my wants, needs, and life to Your care. Be glorified through my sorrow. Deliver me as only You can. Bless and transform my future. I trust You, Jesus.

Square One

If you're in a desperate new beginning or back to square one...

Will it be hard? Yes. Will it be worth it? Yes.

Can you do it? *Oh, yes.*

Part II

God's Financial Therapy for Your Financial Wounds

HEAL THE HURTS

Chapter Five

GOD'S FINANCIAL THERAPY

When I began my career as a wealth advisor, I thought my work would be about managing money. I was so wrong.

Whenever my clients' needs were directly related to money, I was well-prepared and ready with solutions. I soon realized, however, that my work would be as much about managing emotions and memories as it was about managing money.

A solid investment process is a relatively straightforward matter. The healing of financial wounds is a whole lot more complicated.

Yet I had a hard time finding a single client whose relationship with wealth hadn't been shaped, skewed, or soured by an emotional wound from the past.

Three core factors were at work within my dear, highly accomplished clientele:

1. No one escapes financial disappointment. Financial wounds happen to us all.
2. Until we process unresolved wounds, we financially overcompensate.
3. We are easily triggered when a current situation reminds us of our painful past.

As a registered investment advisor, I found that third factor to be the most treacherous.

It became obvious to me that buried emotions rear their ugly heads in the way we interact with wealth. This made me wonder: what about me? Am I exempt? Aside from the financial ups and downs we all experience, what is my financial wound? And how is it affecting my personal relationship with money?

One quiet day of self-reflection and a pen was all I needed. I wrote about my childhood and my past. Before long, my emotional wound with money poured from my gut and onto the page. I hadn't thought about it—consciously, that is—for years. Like my clients, I'd glossed over it. But on that day, I finally knew the "why" of my own financial peculiarities.

Thankfully, like you, I'm a person of faith in Jesus Christ. And by God's grace, He showed me what to do next. In the following three chapters, I'm going to help you do the same.

A Childhood Trauma

At nine years old, I was enthralled by every finishing designer touch and the beauty of our magnificent home. By second grade, I knew I wanted to be an interior designer when I grew up.

But then the wolves came and took it away.

The designer rug was pulled out from under us when a tall sheriff rang our doorbell. I'd never seen a sheriff up close before. I peered at him from a safe distance behind my mother's skirt, holding my breath, hoping he'd be nice. He was. He spoke quietly, a few polite words, and gently handed her a paper. My mother crumpled into tears. And that night came the wolves…

At my mother's apparent invitation, six unshaven strangers who really did look like wolves to this panicked little girl, arrived in dirty pickup trucks to invade our beautiful house.

Their mission: to remove all contents in two days. At that point, according to the sheriff's paper, the state would demolish our home to build an expressway.

Years earlier, my parents had sold our house to the state of New York for an eye-popping price. But when politics stalled their massive, multicity highway project, my parents stalled our move. Why not continue living here free for as long as possible until the state sorted it all out?

Several years passed, and the state still made no contact. My hardworking parents finally invested the house proceeds in our family business.

And then they divorced.

My father left the state for a new business, and my mother reluctantly rushed in to take over our business. In her early thirties, it was her first real job, which she bravely undertook while learning basic skills like how to drive a car and write a check. With enviable faith and remarkable grit, she scrambled to take over our sophisticated business enterprise.

Her exhaustive efforts were locked on one thing only: to hold back financial ruin.

But that was not to be.

An unthinkable criminal act ushered in the final blow to our financial survival.

Arsonists set fire to our business—which was uninsured—torching whatever crumbs of security might have remained. I vividly remember the five-alarm blaze as we raced to the scene, billowing orange flames shooting to the sky.

It was the cremation of my childhood.

With the total loss of our business and income, all we had left was our house.

And now the sheriff was telling us we had to leave.

With two days until demolition, there was no time for boxes or packing. It was too late to plan anything.

This was a grab-and-go situation, and with disturbing gusto, they did.

I watched silently as the wolf-men rifled through our belongings and removed our furniture. Tears flowed as they took away my beloved piano and my pink bicycle. Nothing was spared, not even my dolls, toys, or games. They carried off the contents of my entire world.

And they didn't stop there. Like wolves at a frenzied feast, after emptying our house, they yanked plumbing and electrical fixtures hard from walls and floors. The sights and sounds were jarring and awful. Unimaginable suffering was inflicted upon my beloved home that traumatic night.

At the end of forty-eight brutal hours, our house stood dark and eerily quiet. There was nothing left. No contents. No fixtures. No plumbing. No life. All was gone forever. For reasons unknown to me, I never saw my belongings again.

A Tender Understanding of Our Peculiar Ways

As I scribbled my story with surprising intensity, I uncovered the reason why I grew up to loathe any lack of planning. I know firsthand the terrible, unthinkable financial sorrows that can happen to those who don't plan. Please, don't let it happen to you.

I also realized why I'm driven to work so hard, save so passionately, and, above all, not allow myself to be financially dependent on any person. As the lightning bolt of understanding pierced my heart, I felt God's presence. And I understood why I am ever tender in all matters of home.

Then, I turned my attention to my husband, wondering if I might connect his childhood to his financial style. What were his financial wounds?

At nine, his widowed mother was impoverished by his father's early death. There was no money. Kind friends often dropped off bags of food at their door. As the oldest of six little boys, he was designated as the new "head of the household." He went to work before and after elementary school to help feed his family.

His generous-hearted mother often took in needy families, sharing with strangers the food he'd fought so hard to buy. Years later, as a teenager, he worked at an exclusive country club, parking luxury automobiles for wealthy club members who scorned him as unworthy to date their daughters.

When we examine our financial wounds, our attitudes, emotions, and behavior around money begin to make sense. I was filled with new compassion for my dear husband's unique financial perspective.

Childhood trauma sears a child's subconscious like grill marks on tender meat and later informs their adult interactions with money. For each of us, it happens differently. But, as believers, we share a decisive advantage: we do not have to carry the weight of old financial baggage into our future. The Lord understands our financial pain. And He wants to help us overcome it.

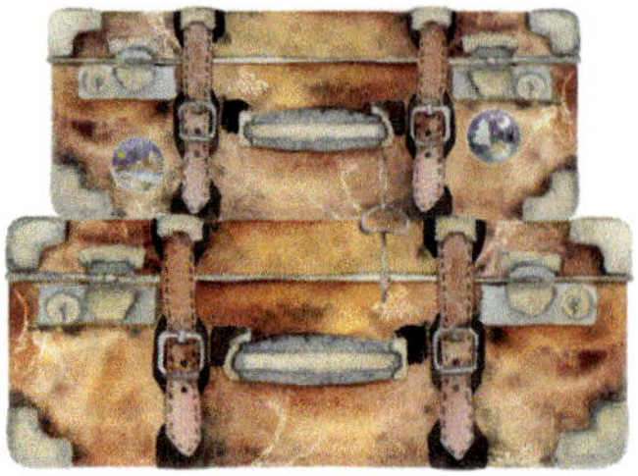

I'd been struggling to figure out how to make clients feel financially safe. That day, I realized what they needed—and it had nothing to do with money. Here it is: we need God's financial therapy for our financial wounds.

Does Your Relationship with Wealth Express Truth—or Damage?

Do you ever feel financially blocked…by a wound, mistake, or regret?

Do you find yourself in a dismal financial mood despite a desirable net worth?

Do you wrestle with anger, unforgiveness, financial grief, or other unresolved issues?

Much of our financial frustration and unhappiness festers from old, unresolved hurts and trauma, some recent, others going back to childhood. Memories lurk beneath our subconscious, springing out during any situation that echoes our painful past.

Why, you may ask, is this a problem for me? My wealth story is one of abundance and sufficiency—not of suffering.

But when our truest values are buried alive beneath an unhealed injury, what we're expressing through our wealth is *not a reflection of truth, but of damage.*

Too many of us have wealth without joy, without peace, without calm, without purpose.

Until you are unblocked—set free—you'll repeat unconscious patterns of thought and behavior. These have held you back from God's fullest financial flow. I've seen more people sabotage the blessings of wealth than I can ever count. Why limit God's purpose in your life?

Here's my recommendation:

- Search for anything interfering with your chance to live a wealth-blessed life.
- Isolate your wound, name it, and quarantine it.

- Offer your wound—and offer your whole self—to Him for cleansing, so you may seal the wound forever.

If we let Him, God can free and heal us from our injuries as we...

- ...confront our wounds
- ...speak His truth into them
- ...forgive all the parties concerned—including ourselves

Mission Possible

You really can retrofit your financial disposition and produce a different financial future. This is "mission possible."

If you need extra help resolving deeply grooved emotions, please see a licensed mental health professional, which I am not. It's always wise to seek counsel whenever needed. For certain troublesome issues, I highly recommend you talk it out with a professional.

In my experience with countless clients and friends, I've noticed that in certain milder cases, exposing and examining the roots of our financial peculiarities seems to be enough to help us make new, life-freeing decisions and step confidently into a new resolve.

This new awareness is like flipping a switch and turning on the Light. You'll be surprised how many breakthroughs can be yours before you finish the last page of this book.

I've seen so many people overcome persistent financial issues and become free and unbound. You can retrain your auto-response system to enjoy a holy, elegant, and purposeful relationship with wealth.

Let's invite God into your wealth story.

By shoring up and reinforcing a new inner foundation, you can build a new wealth structure on spiritually blessed and solid ground that will outlast the storms of life.

A Search-and-Destroy Mission

Let's undertake a search-and-destroy mission to uncover any unhealed financial wounds blocking your wealth-blessed future. Together, we'll gently expose and clean out old hurts causing you present financial distress.

I'm not a therapist—but God is.

He will perform His financial therapy.

And I will hold your hand.

May the healing process begin. You'll understand your financial self in a way you never did before. Yes, the past informs the future—but it will no longer control it. For God has His purpose for the wealth He flows through our lives, and you don't want to miss it.

Prepare to be surprised at how free and unblocked you can become. When you shine a light into darkness, there is nowhere for old wounds to hide. We can examine our past with courage and confidence because the One who loves us can redeem anything. He will tenderly care for our wounds, if we let Him.

Money talks. It tells our secrets. So, let's find out what you've been whispering to yourself. Are you ready to unblock your flow?

Chapter Six

GOD CAN HEAL YOUR PAST

Here is a sampling of common wounds I encountered with clients. For each wound, we'll examine the financial risks associated with that wound, and, more importantly, what you can do about it.

Poor Childhood

Did you have a poor childhood? Good thing you have a rich Father. Nothing exists that He doesn't own. And you are His heir. Hold your head high, for you've been adopted into royalty. You have an inheritance waiting for you, and some of that inheritance may just be distributed while you're here on earth.

"And you also were included in Christ when you heard the message of truth, the gospel of your salvation. When you believed, you were marked in him with a seal, the promised Holy Spirit, who is a deposit guaranteeing our inheritance until the redemption of those who are God's possession—to the praise of his glory" (Ephesians 1:13-14).

"I pray that the eyes of your heart may be enlightened in order that you may know the hope to which he has called you, the riches of his glorious inheritance in his holy people and his incomparably great power for us who believe..." (Ephesians 1:18-19a).

Financial Risks of a Poor Childhood

Sometimes, we merge our perceptions of the past, present, and future and adopt them all into one financial identity. You had a rough start. You don't have to have a rough finish. Not if you stay close to your Father.

What You Can Do

Refine your concept of what it means to be wealth-blessed:

My soul is my most important asset.

I am rich in Christ.

I have come far…and am going far.

Sin and Mistakes

If you've made a financial mistake, welcome to humanity.

Your financial mistakes don't make you noteworthy; they make you normal.

Some of our mistakes have been so large, we don't believe we can recover this side of Heaven. Do you think wealth-blessed Christians have never made a mistake? Of course, they have and will continue to do so.

Financial Risk of Sin and Mistakes

We often drag our past financial indiscretions around like a sack of spoiled potatoes, weighing us down and stinking up our lives. Who has time to contemplate God's punishment when we've been doing such a great job punishing ourselves?

We become judge and jury, wearing past financial mistakes as a cloak of shame. We deem them evidence of our unworthiness, proof of our wretchedness. This is a bunch of made-up theology not rooted in God's Word.

What You Can Do

The Father declares that if you make a mistake—even a big one—your whole life is not a mistake. You just have to ask the right Person for forgiveness. If you ask Him, He will forgive you. And unlike you, He will forget your sin.

Forgiveness is the showcase of God's grace. Forgiveness of financial sin is not outside the boundaries of God's promise to you and me if we'll only ask with a pure and contrite heart. Your sins can be separated as far from you as the east is from the west if you only ask. So, ask!

Shame

Shame is an insidious wound that infiltrates your mind and damages your finances—even when the cause of your shame is unfounded. What's worse is that there is no way to diagnose shame except by its symptoms.

Shame distorts your otherwise logical reasoning and reduces you to feeling small, like a nobody. But according to God, you are a big somebody.

You need not prove yourself to anyone.

Never allow shame to direct your financial decisions.

Financial Risks of Shame

As I've shared, my husband's family was very poor when he was a teenager. On one occasion, he wanted to date a girl, but her father refused because of his poverty.

Sixty years later, though successful and shame-free, for some reason, he resists negotiating the price of anything. I've often wondered if he may need to affirm to himself and to the salesperson that he can now afford to pay full price.

See what I mean? Even the tiniest residue of shame will peek out at times that mimic past events. As I said, we can only diagnose shame by its symptoms.

Think carefully. Is any financial shame from your past harming your financial future?

Since shame—often unwarranted—will rear its ugly head at some point in most of our lives, isn't it best we learn to notice and address it right now?

What You Can Do

Shame is a feeling based on "bad intel"—by that, I mean inferior, outdated, inaccurate intelligence fed into your mind.

How do we overcome bad intel? With good intel. With truth.

Read God's truths daily, directly from the Bible. Claim His promises.

If needed, talk to a therapist and especially to the Holy Therapist: the Lord, who can change you in an instant, fill you with Truth, and make your mindset brand new.

Reboot your financial self-talk. Always be ready to draw a line in the sand and say to your wandering esteem, "This far and no farther."

Renouncing shame will take practice and repetition. That well-grooved shame response is deep and dark. You may have to speak out loud to your mirror. And read to yourself a carefully chosen, precisely targeted, well-worded statement of truth—daily—along with Bible scriptures written in your own hand.

I do.

Examples of Carefully Worded Statements to Renounce Shame

"I am loved, wanted, and safe."

"If I am loved by God, who can unsettle me by not loving me?"

Examples of Scriptures to Renounce Shame

"Do not be afraid; you will not be put to shame. Do not fear disgrace; you will not be humiliated. You will forget the shame of your youth..." (Isaiah 54:4a).

"For the Holy Spirit, God's gift, does not want you to be afraid of people, but to be wise and strong, and to love them and enjoy being with them" (2 Timothy 1:7 TLB).

Sadness

Some of us carry a heavy load of lingering financial sadness throughout our lives. We think we're hiding it, but sadness is a weight that sags our very countenance. Sadness weighs down more than just our faces but also our finances.

Financial Risks of Sadness

When we just need to feel a little better, and to comfort ourselves, we often turn to spending. There's even a name for it: retail therapy. But retail therapy is no therapy at all.

It costs far more and does far less than genuine therapy. Its comfort lasts only moments. Its promised cure is fake, like an anesthetic that wears off shortly after you unwrap the purchase.

Until we interrupt the damaging pattern of hurting, spending, comforting, then, hurting again, spending as therapy becomes our auto-response that disrupts, disappoints, and undermines the framework of our otherwise smart financial decisions. It becomes a difficult habit to break because it drugs us with a very short-lived high, followed by a cruel return to the same low state of being as before. And it delays the delivery of genuine relief.

You don't deserve cruelty. Not to your finances and not to your life.

What You Can Do

Is your sadness a season? Or a lifestyle?

If it's a season, such as after the death of a loved one, you may be engulfed in the early stages of grief. This can create a mental fog that impedes sound decision-making. Be at peace, my friend, and ask someone to pray with you daily. Avoid spending decisions for one year past your sadness—or until your pain has subsided, your heartache well-managed, and your emotional recovery well underway.

But if sadness is your *lifestyle*, if it *never* goes away, you must take even greater care to prevent it from robbing you of your financial strength and dignity. In sadness, you may think you have nothing left to lose—but, in fact, God will tell you that if you are alive, you have much more to give.

The one who most wants to comfort you in your sadness is God.

Search the scriptures for His transforming words. Search your heart for answers.

Search for an understanding therapist. Search for friends to engage.

Self-Pity

Self-pity is sadness gone off the rails. And we're all subject to bouts of it. Here is not Heaven, that's for sure. People hurt one another. Abandon one another. Betray one another.

You may have been rejected—or ejected—from a great job or a great life. You may be enduring an unspeakable loss or an unjust expense, one you feel you can never overcome.

Grief is a clean and noble reaction to sorrow and loss. We can expect to feel sadness from time to time. But self-pity is our refusal to let God have His way in our life.

Financial Risks of Self-Pity

The financial risks of self-pity are so overwhelming that there is no room to name them here, but deep down, you know how self-pity is compromising your life.

What You Can Do

Do this to make an immediate difference:

Take every thought captive (for extra support, see 2 Corinthians 10:3-5).

Capture runaway self-pitying self-talk, and compress these thoughts tightly so they cannot do more damage to your financial life and happiness. Trust God to hold you up when your hope sags. He will set you on a high rock, so you will not be swept away by the pitiful rushing waters below.

This is not easy, but He wants to lift you out of self-pity. Reach for him.

Pessimism

A funny thing about pessimism. Pessimism invites defeat.

It establishes defeat as our default setpoint. It functions like a dare we make to God to prove us wrong and intervene for us. He is unimpressed and under no compulsion to prove Himself to deliberately faithless children.

Financial Risks of Pessimism

Pessimism ruins financial happiness. It stops God's flow. It robs you of joy and hope. It makes your days dreary and your nights impossible. It lures you to numb your insistent sorrow via unhealthy means.

Pessimism costs you socially, too, acting as a repellent to those who might like to socialize or do business with you but who stay away because of the energy drain of your perennially sour outlook.

What You Can Do

1. Talk (Talking is different from griping.)

    - Talk to a friend. Tell them you've decided to change.
    - Talk to people you admire who have a sunny disposition and navigate life successfully. Ask them their secret. You might be surprised at their answer.
    - Talk to your pastor about your commitment to a new uplift in attitude.
    - Talk to a therapist if needed. Your pessimism may reflect a protective coating over past disappointments you've been unable to resolve on your own.

2. Pray

    - Surrender your mood to the Lord.
    - Ask God to change your outlook and disposition.
    - Read and claim His Word.

Unlovedness

If you feel unloved, I want to wrap my arms around you in a healing embrace. If you were an unloved child, my arms are already reaching for you.

But unlovedness is a lie. You are not bereft. You are beloved. That's the truth.

Like an artisan counting every thread of a woven masterpiece, God has counted the very hairs on our heads. The God of the Universe loves you more than any human ever could and has made it possible for you to have a personal relationship with Him through His Son, Jesus. He's been whispering to you for some time, and you feel His presence now. He longs for intimate communion with you.

Financial Risks of Unlovedness

The financial risks of unlovedness make me want to cry because the things you buy will never replace the love you need. A material item cannot hug you or love you. But how might your spending change if you believed you were deeply loved? Wouldn't you need a little less from the outside if you felt more loved on the inside?

What You Can Do

If you long to feel loved, stop spending and start reading... the New Testament. Begin with the gospels and read right through to the letters. Drink in God's love. Fill yourself up with truth.

So much of the hurt and angst we try to medicate through overspending and acquisition can be solved by a simple decision to live in the truth of God, which means to live life loved. Your Father sent His only Son, so you might be forgiven of sin and enter an intimate Father-child relationship with Him. Jesus gave His life for you. *"But God demonstrates his own love for us in this: While we were still sinners, Christ died for us"* (Romans 5:8).

Even if you don't have family or friends, you are not bereft. You are beloved. Loved and cherished children don't need so much from the outside, for they feel full on the inside.

Smallness of Identity

Humility is essential. Smallness is a lie.

Whether your birth parents knew it or not, your life is by no accident. God chose you to come into this world. The Bible affectionately tells us God knitted you together in your mother's womb. He was there as your body was being formed in secret. He knew you before you were born. All the days ordained for you were written in His book before one of them came to be (Psalm 139:13-16). Your fingerprint—indeed, your very life-print—is unique.

Small identity? Not you.

Financial Risks of a Small Identity

When we believe our lives are small, we're tempted to spend money on large purchases to make our lives feel larger.

One dear client, a wealthy divorcee in her sixties, remarried a lovely man, who was a perfect match for her in every way, except he lacked the professional credentials of her social peer group. Though he loved her, he felt small, inadequate, and anguished when introduced to her circle of friends. Together, they concocted a revised and more impressive background so he could combat his small identity. He rehearsed and mastered his lines until he almost believed them. But despite the smooth words he spoke on the outside, he still felt small on the inside.

So, he fought his sense of "smallness" by insisting they live large. They sold her upscale, but conservative waterfront condominium and built a grand home. He still felt small.

So, they bought luxury automobiles and replaced them annually. He still felt small.

So, they turned to art, spending lavishly on pieces not appreciated even by their most sophisticated friends. But no matter how grandly they spent, he still felt small.

In the end, they spent it all.

Millions of dollars were squandered on creating an artificially big life to escape feeling small. If only they'd read what God says about the matter.

What You Can Do

When you feel large inside, you don't have to spend money to create largeness outside you. The counteracting decision is to live life loved. A well-loved child doesn't feel crushed by their smallness—but is, in fact, cherished for it.

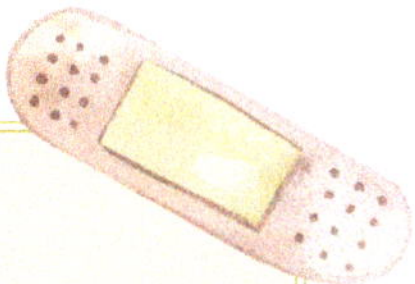

Wound Recovery Checklist

1. Confront your wound. Call it by name.
2. Be alert to triggers that remind you of it. They will be unique to you.
3. Avoid tempting situations. Know your enemy: the enemy of your soul will try to exploit any situation that echoes your negative past.
4. Speak truth to yourself. Affirm your identity in Christ.
5. Ask God to heal you, layer by layer.
6. Make a conscious decision to live life loved. Write it down. Read it daily.
7. Forge ahead with confidence, moving forward, not backward, by taking little steps to live in truth and grace.

Chapter Seven

GOD CAN HEAL YOUR PRESENT

Unforgiveness

Many of us have wrestled with financial forgiveness—including me. I was once swindled out of an entire year's salary. Unfair as it seems, unforgiveness is an impediment to wealth. Infuriating, isn't it? Why should we, the victims, have to pay the price for somebody else's wrongdoing?

But God requires us to forgive our offenders. I find it outrageous—but then, He is God, and I am not.

Adding to our outrage is that, unlike other types of sins that fall into nebulous and, therefore, forgivable territory, financial sins are not like that. Financial sins are concrete. If someone insults us, for example, we can ponder whether they meant harm—or only misspoke. With non-financial offenses, we have wiggle room to speculate whether the offense was major or minor, intentional or accidental.

But money sins are measurable. The damage of financial injury is quantifiable.

If a parent didn't provide for you, if a friend stole from you, if an employer cheated you, there's no mulling over whether the offense was real or imagined. These assaults are precise.

The person who financially sinned against you owes a debt, one they may never repay.

But consider this: There was a third party present at the time of your financial injustice.

He is the Lord. He was watching, waiting, hoping the other party would use their free will to make the right choice.

When they didn't, He was furious. Scripture promises it is so (Matthew 25:45-46 and Psalm 105:15). Beware to the person who hurt you, for God's fury comes with a thunder that reverberates through the heavens. There is no escaping His judgment and His punishment without repentance, which is on them, not on you. Your financial adversary's ill-gotten gain is a rock around their neck, an anchor that will drown them unless they ask for and receive God's mercy and forgiveness.

What are you, the injured party, supposed to do in the meantime? Can you have peace and openness with God without releasing your grip on the unforgiveness you feel they deserve? Unfortunately, no.

"But if you do not forgive others their sins, your Father will not forgive your sins" (Matthew 6:15).

But do not despair. Forgiveness comes only from God. He alone can release a sinner from their deserved fate. Our part of the forgiveness process is to release the sinner from our unforgiving grip, hand the debt they owe us over to the Lord, and let God have His way.

Financial Risks of Unforgiveness

We mistakenly believe that unless we find a way to justify the offense, we can find no grounds to forgive it. But with financial sins, these types of mental gyrations are fruitless. No sane person can pretend we weren't cheated, harmed, or financially victimized.

So, we stay stuck in the bondage of unforgiveness, locked in a protective steel suit that allows no breath, growth, or grace for our own lives.

Instead of breaking free, we...

- overspend defiantly.
- numb ourselves with hyperactivity.
- adopt a jaded outlook to brace ourselves against future assaults.
- hold onto all future resources tightly so it won't happen again.

Without forgiveness, no matter how much wealth enters our lives, our painful past will sneak in along with it. Without forgiveness, financial happiness has no chance.

What You Can Do

Unforgiveness is carrying the burden of suffering from an unpaid debt. I suggest you hand that debt to the Lord. Let Him deal with the offender. Get out of the way.

You don't have to let them off the hook. Just hand that hook to the Lord.

Free yourself from the chokehold another's sin has around your financial neck. After you've handed their debt to God, you'll be free. If God is the judge—not you—the matter will be handled justly. If the one who sinned against you genuinely repents (and keep in mind, there is no fooling God), they'll find His forgiveness.

God will not be mocked (Galatians 6:7). His forgiveness cannot be manipulated. There is no way a swindler can swindle God.

So, don't worry about fairness. God can take care of Himself. And God can take care of you. What happened to you may have been intolerable and may be unforgivable. But once you're free, you'll reopen the channel for the Lord's financial happiness and blessing.

How to free yourself? Two steps:

1. First, grieve. Grieving is a clean and honorable process that precedes forgiveness.
2. Then, forgive.

Hard? No—impossible.

And you can do it. Let it go.

Comparison to Others

Side-view mirrors are great for cars. But bad for people. Comparison with others is a trap that will not just foster discontent, but also rob you of wealth. Comparison muddies judgment, leading us to make financial decisions based on deceitful criteria.

As a financial advisor entrusted with the most private details of my clients' lives, I learned that no one really knows another person's financial status from the outside—or even necessarily from the inside. Tax returns and financial statements tell only part of the story. Until we see and know every financial detail of that person's life, we're lacking key unknowns that deeply impact their financial reality.

Some of my clients appeared quite well off on paper, with seven-figure annual incomes—yet I held my breath at their spending. Other clients appeared on financial statements to have only modest financial means—but the only thing modest was their spending. They were the most financially secure of all.

Financial Risks of Comparison

If you're governed by a need to compare yourself to another or if you're in a race to prove who has the most, exit that race now. You deserve better than what you'll get in any such entanglement. Trying to build esteem based on the illusion of superiority is a fool's game.

The risks of comparison are profound and promise unrelenting discontent, mental fatigue from keeping up, and generalized lowness of life. All this as your wealth is being drained to show someone who may not even notice or care.

What You Can Do

God made you, fashioned you, and formed you for His pleasure. You will know yourself and will be thankful for who you are when you finally see yourself through His eyes.

Get a hacksaw and cut off the side view mirror. Eyes straight ahead on your own path.

Go ahead and prove yourself with money—but not to anyone else, but God.

Rebellion

As we seek to put childhood behind us, financial rebellion is often our last frontier.

We refuse to do whatever we don't want to do. And just like a two-year-old, we want what we want, and we want it now. Don't dare try to give us financial counsel, even if you know about money and you love us.

Outwardly, our body looks all grown-up, but inwardly we seethe like a toddler in a tantrum.

Financial Risks of Rebellion

Consider how a spirit of rebellion has financially impacted you. Is it giving you what you want in the way of relationships? And money? Has it increased wealth? Happiness? Holiness?

Or has it stopped God's flow? Cost you work? Customers? Relationships?

If you're self-employed, are your clients staying with you and referring you to their friends? Or are you confronting arguments, broken relationships, and accusations everywhere you turn? Do you foresee any realistic way rebellion is going to help you get what you need and long for?

What You Can Do

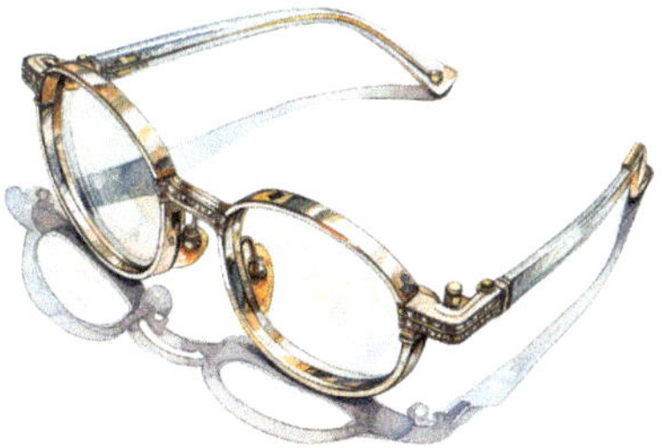

Look back to an earlier time of peace and acceptance. What happened that fostered a spirit of rebellion within you? Was it a defensive reaction to unfairness? Is there something or someone you need to forgive?

You're an adult now. You are in charge of your life. You cannot depend on—or blame—anyone else for the financial decisions you make today.

Sacrifice your rebellion at the altar. Ask God for His forgiveness, strength, and help. Read scriptures. Surrender your spirit and your whole life to His Lordship. Give everything to Him, for no matter your past, He can make your path straight. He will help you make up for the time you lost, because the path of the upright is a highway.

"The way of the sluggard is blocked with thorns, but the path of the upright is a highway" (Proverbs 15:19).

Apologize to your loved ones and ask for forgiveness for the price they've had to pay for your rebellion. Demonstrate your new outlook in a verifiable way, perhaps by taking on a task or job you previously resisted.

If you own a business, take bold action with everyone concerned to make things right. Humble yourself, and trust that in due time, God will lift you up (James 4:10).

Envy

Many of us—okay, arguably all of us—wrestle against false idols that continuously surround and tempt us. But if your envy is financially rooted, stay on high alert.

Don't think of envy as green. Think of it as Code Red. Because jealousy is akin to murder. Envy is a curse on your life that will crush your chances to be wealth-blessed.

Financial Risks of Envy

Envy will tempt you to spend on what does not satisfy. Envy will drain your wallet.

Envy will exhaust you. Envy will twist your life into a contortion of your former financial self. Envy will keep financial happiness from coming anywhere near you.

Envy is a sin.

What You Can Do

If you feel envy for another person's financial resources, jump up and down to stamp it out with the same urgency you'd use to extinguish a fire in your home. Imagine a stack of important papers on your desk catching fire. You'd rush into immediate action, throwing everything you have against that fire to extinguish it before the rest of your house goes up in flames. That's how you must treat the smallest spark of financial jealousy, for its flame will engulf your whole financial life and push godly wealth far from you.

You do not know why you have more than one and less than another. You do not know God's plan for your future. You cannot state conclusively His plan for you. His ways are higher than our ways. We can pray—and we should.

But envy? A hard no.

Not now, not ever. Period.

Grumbling and Perfectionism

Oh dear. If you are a perfectionist, I'm afraid you were born on the wrong planet. This world will never get it right. Expect to be chronically disappointed.

Thankfully, He assures us that though we live in this imperfect world, we are not of the world. We can adopt contentment as our new normal, leap over disappointments, and change our financial temperament—yes, we really can.

Perfectionism has a wayward daughter named Grumbling, which delivers a slow drip of emotionally convenient relief every time we press the tongue lever. But grumbling is a placebo providing no actual relief. It's useless for changing our circumstances. It will *not* help us gain what we seek. Worse, it does nothing to motivate God to rescue us.

I know this because I am a former world-class grumbler. And I was defensive about it. I thought grumbling was evidence of a reasonable mind. After all…

…isn't it obvious when something is wrong?

…isn't it observant to identify the part of a thing that's not perfect?

…isn't it smart of me to locate that one imperfect piece of an otherwise perfect whole?

But grumbling comes from a heart that refuses to be fully satisfied. Grumbling may briefly motivate someone to give you something you want, but it won't budge God one speck in your favor.

He is decidedly annoyed at grumbling. He's pleased by thanks and gratitude that ignores the missing parts. He's pleased by prayer, the kind in which we ask for what we need and then choose to trust His Lordship.

Financial Risks of Grumbling and Perfectionism

Aside from angering God, grumbling turns off those much-needed people who might otherwise want to help you. Grumblers do not retain the loyal support of others for very long. No one has enough spare energy to please an unpleasable person. Ingratitude and the constant measuring of what's wrong instead of what's right is not a path to popularity—or lasting financial success.

In fact, grumbling widens the gap between where you are and where you hope to go. For proof, ask the Israelites in the desert. Ask Moses. Grumblers displease God, the owner of all financial assets in the world.

When I first entered into an active relationship with Christ, little did I realize how well-grooved was my cozy rut of grumbling and perfectionism. Why, I was near perfect at pointing out all the imperfections around me. I meant no harm or heavenly disrespect. My intentions felt modest, humble, reasonable. And smart—very smart.

Then I read Philippians 2:14-16. *"Do everything without grumbling or arguing, so that you may become blameless and pure, 'children of God without fault in a warped and crooked generation.' Then you will shine among them like stars in the sky as you hold firmly to the word of life."*

Ouch.

What You Can Do

Do what I did. Ask yourself why you became a perfectionist. Children aren't born that way. Just watch them play—or eat.

Maybe you had a critical or absent parent, an overbearing teacher, or an unreasonable coach. Maybe you lived through a time in which you lacked security.

One reason I grumbled was to equalize myself among others. I feared they might think my blessings were too good and would stop caring and praying for me.

Try to discern *where* this spirit of grumbling came from. Spray the antiseptic of forgiveness all over your infected wound, and then surrender it to the Lord. This will please Him very much. From my personal experience, there's only one way I know, following repentance and forgiveness, to break the financial cycle of grumbling:

- Try a thirty-day fast from all grumbling, discontent, and perfectionism.
- If you can't make it all the way through, try seven days. If not, try one day.
- One day at a time. And paste Philippians 2:14-16 where you can see it.

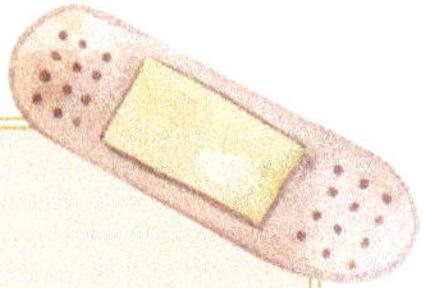

Wound Recovery Checklist

1. Confront your wound. Call it by name.
2. Be alert to triggers that remind you of it. They will be unique to you.
3. Avoid tempting situations. Know your enemy: the enemy of your soul will try to exploit any situation that echoes your negative past.
4. Speak truth to yourself. Affirm your identity in Christ.
5. Ask God to heal you, layer by layer.
6. Make a conscious decision to live life loved. Write it down. Read it daily.
7. Forge ahead with confidence, moving forward, not backward, by taking little steps to live in truth and grace.

Chapter Eight

GOD CAN HEAL YOUR FUTURE

Get-Rich-Quick Mindset

You don't think you have enough time to acquire the wealth you want and need. You're running out of time, energy, and options, and now you've drifted into a get-rich-quick mindset.

Logical, right? On the surface, it appears so.

But God is a get-rich-slow kind of God. He owns time. Calendars are meaningless to Him. He can accomplish more than we'd dare to ask or even dream of in any timeframe He chooses.

Financial Risks of a Get-Rich-Quick Mindset

Scripture says it better than I can.

". . . but the man who wants to get rich quick will quickly fall" (Proverbs 28:20).

"Trying to get rich quick is evil and leads to poverty" (Proverbs 28:22).

One way some people try to get rich quickly is by gambling. Why is this a curse? Because, games of chance elevate "chance" to become your god.

What You Can Do

Stay away from every form of get-rich-quick. Consider switching to the alternative approach of get-wisdom-quick.

Reluctance to Work

For you, work is a four-letter word. Someone may have even accused you of being lazy.

But I don't think you're lazy. I think you're scared. Trapped. Conflicted. Maybe even heartbroken.

I grieve with you for whatever is behind your sorrow. God grieves with you, too. Do you not feel it?

Now it's true: Scripture is full of the risks of the lazy. A lazy person is thought to be a fool. But would a lazy person bother to read this book? I don't think so.

If you're scared, let me help you find your courage. It's time to confront the basis of your resistance to work. Let's be brave and uncover your wound.

Perhaps you were hurt when a parent chose work over you. You felt they loved work more than they loved you, that their job was more important than the precious job of spending time with you. You felt rejected. Unimportant. Shoved aside in the name of a work project or a client. Or perhaps you watched a parent surrender their health or their very life to overwork, working harder than anyone should be forced to work, even to the point of exhaustion, illness, or death.

Or, you may know someone unhappy in their work, but bound and constrained by it.

Or, you may have seen someone you care about mistreated, mishandled, or shoved aside at the end of a loyal tenure of service, and you don't want to be that person—that victim.

I understand.

You may say, "I don't have to take care of myself, and I won't. I am trusting God to do it." But aren't we to seek the dignity of employment? Did God not tell us to work?

Work is ordained by God.

Through work, we find our calling. We discover the depth of our talents.

Through work, we're refined into the wonderful person God made us to be. We make new friendships and may even meet our future loved ones.

Through work, we bless and are blessed. Through work, we create value—and value creates wealth.

If God has given you the ability to earn wealth, you mustn't squander it. It takes money to fund the cause of Christ, and God may have appointed you with "the ability to earn wealth" for His assigned purposes. Don't hate working for money. Don't turn your back on any gift from God, including the ability to earn wealth.

Financial Risks of Reluctance to Work

Some of these risks are obvious: forced dependence on others and subjugation to their choices if they are the ones funding your lifestyle. But also consider this: inaction can cause depression. *"Sluggards do not plow in season; so at harvest time they look but find nothing"* (Proverbs 20:4).

Maybe you think you're only inactive because of depression. But what if you're only depressed because you're inactive?

What You Can Do

I don't want you to "find nothing." Find something. What is your inaction costing you?

Clearly, it blocks God's financial flow.

But beyond money, have you counted all the other costs of a reluctance to work? Freedom? Mental peace? Spiritual self-acceptance? A sense of accomplishment and purpose over your life?

What seems like laziness is often a paralyzing fear of moving forward. But we dare not admit it, so we mask our passivity by claiming to be "waiting on God."

Admit your fears to the Father. He knows you're afraid. He'll fill the frightened space with new courage if you only ask. Pray. Ask God for forgiveness, strength, and help. Claim and recite aloud His promises.

Seek counsel from godly people you respect about where you might turn. Talk to a friend, mentor, pastor, or therapist. Talk lovingly to yourself.

Start somewhere, anywhere. Tell others you are now actively available for work.

Know this: blessings await you in your work.

Confusion

Are you confused about money? Of course, you are. How could you not be confused?

We're bombarded with an overload of financial information coming at us around the clock from everywhere. Much of it is irrelevant to our personal situation or motivated by sales angles of which we are unaware.

We can drive ourselves crazy and learn too much—yet still not know enough to do ourselves any good. No wonder we live in confusion.

There's just way too much information out there.

Our inbox is invaded daily by uninvited "financial experts" who all disagree with one another. We could spend every waking and sleeping hour reading about finance from these insistent experts from all over the planet, all disagreeing on what you should do and how you should proceed.

When you look beyond their vastly differing "success formulas," one common denominator is that they're all grounded in some kind of principle or paradigm.

They all have an agenda. But what is it?

Often, it's to sell or promote a product that will benefit them, not you. After all, remember, they don't know you.

Often, they promote a secret financial process or a mysterious theory. Sign up right away...so they can gather private financial information about you, keep you hooked and watching, and grow themselves as influencers. This is how advertisers pay them.

Admittedly, sometimes their theory is sincere, based on a passionate belief. They mean no harm. But wolves in sheep's clothing can cause great harm to you.

Financial Risks of Confusion

Confusion makes us financially vulnerable. When differing advice comes from many sources, we often select the one coming either from the nicest person (who may be insincere), or the smoothest talker (who may be a criminal).

One reason the legendary financial swindler, Bernie Madoff, was so effective was because he made wealth and investing seem simple. He promised his clients a crazy high investment return, and "confirmed" their stellar results via his special quarterly statements.

A client showed me one of Madoff's statements. I was speechless. It was oh-so-simple—so as to avoid confusion. No assets were listed. Only the client's starting figure, ending figure, and amount of increase for the quarter. A third grader could have done as good a job writing that statement.

"This is outrageous," I said. "There's no information here at all! What assets do you actually own through Madoff?"

"Ahh," my client nodded in the hushed tone of an enthusiastic insider. "That's part of his secret process. He sells all the assets right before the statement."

What? I stared at him as if trying to reason with an insane person. It was obvious to me my otherwise smart and extremely well-educated client was being swindled, although, in those early days, no one could have dreamt of the magnitude of the crime. I suspected enough to beg my client to cease doing business with him. But he turned me down.

"Look," he said. "I trust you more, but he makes more money for me."

My client lost every penny he'd invested with Bernie Madoff. A sad but true story.

What You Can Do

Confusion is one of the easiest financial maladies to fix.

First, strip every so-called "financial concept" down to its core. Since we know for sure that biblical wisdom works, let's start there as our basis for financial truth and direction.

Open your Bible to the Book of Proverbs. There are thirty-one mostly short chapters. Read every one of them, hunting and highlighting every verse that directly—or indirectly—affects money, wealth, earnings, business relationships, or business transactions.

Daily, in addition to your other scriptures, read the Proverbs chapter corresponding to that day of the month. Continue to do that...forever.

Month by month, the Book of Proverbs will equip you with brilliant financial wisdom. It is incredible how five minutes a day can help you become wealth-blessed.

Forsake your old routines that caused confusion, such as reading opinions from internet financial gurus or seeking ungodly advice. Learn God's financial Word for yourself. Know His unconfusing financial truths. Invite Him into your wealth story.

Seek only godly financial counsel from trusted financial advisors. When needed, fast and pray for God's direction and guidance.

Aimless and Stuck

There is one thing even riskier than being aimless and poor. It's being aimless and wealthy.

"For we are God's handiwork, created in Christ Jesus to do good works, which God prepared in advance for us to do" (Ephesians 2:10).

What are you waiting for? Is your talent insufficient? Is your skill inferior? Is your ability subpar? How can you contradict what God Himself knows about you?

Aha. You're blocked by unreasonable fear. And you'd rather not prove your negative opinions correct. He understands.

But inertia is nobody's success formula. It will not move you forward in your finances or in your life. It will not fulfill His ordained purpose for you.

Give yourself to the Lord. Let Him lead you on your path. Be willing to be new at something, less than excellent at first, as you take each step. A wealth-blessed approach pulsates with vitality. Growth and progress are available to you. Step into them.

Financial Risks of Aimlessness

The Bible says it frighteningly well. *"How long will you lie there, you sluggard? When will you get up from your sleep? A little sleep, a little slumber, a little folding of the hands to rest—and poverty will come on you like a bandit and scarcity like an armed man"* (Proverbs 6:9-11).

What You Can Do

Aim low. The very process of aiming and attaining will build your confidence. Gradually, you'll raise your goal and sharpen your aim.

No need to fear taking the wrong path. If you are in the south and want to go north, do you need to define the exact path, route, or timetable at the very start of the journey? No. Just head north! Head north…and, like airline captains flying commercial jetliners at five hundred miles per hour, you will adjust your route as you go. What is your best route? Your exact destination? You won't know that until you begin. Head north!

Impulsive Over-spender

No willpower? Lack of discipline is a curse we put on ourselves.

Free from rules, free from self-discipline, we declare our freedom. Except that kind of freedom is not free at all. We pay a steep price for it. The price we pay is wealth that is not blessed and will not last.

You are far more disciplined than you know. You just didn't realize the stakes were so high and so far-reaching in your future. Few have the discipline to do those things which don't make sense or are outside our genuine longings. But we're all disciplined enough to do those things that bring immediate gratification. Nobody forgets to pick up their winning lottery ticket by 5 p.m.

Life is full of pain. But life is also full of opportunity for freedom. We can have one but not both. No one can choose for us. We must each pick for ourselves if ours will be the pain of discipline—or the pain of regret. Which freedom will you choose?

Financial Risks of Impulsive Overspending

If you think of yourself as an over-spender who lacks impulse control, be prepared that you will live on the edge financially. At some point, you'll be barely making it while others around you have smooth sailing. You may deceive yourself into thinking you're keeping up with everyone else since you spend as much as those who earn twice your pay. But it will be a mirage. In reality, you'll be sinking. What a terribly disadvantaged way to live. Always longing for more is not a blessed way to live.

What You Can Do

Even if your income is in seven figures, spend well under it. The foolish one spends all they get. The wise one saves some for the future. Your thrift will pay off—yes, it really will.

Don't waste your savings. All of us want to feel better. You are not alone in that. The question is, what has the greatest chance of making you feel better?

Fast and pray. And fast from 100 percent of all discretionary shopping for thirty days.

No Bravery after a Failure

Many around you seem to have blessings tumbled onto them, one after another. A friend of yours has started a business growing at rapid-fire speed. Another has a skyrocketing career. It's tempting to envy them. But wealth-blessed Christians know there's no such thing as "all at once." Careers, businesses, and investment accounts take off or rebound after long periods of behind-the-scenes devoted and disciplined attention.

One client took decades to build his business to a respectable level. It leveled off for several years. Then major adversity hit, costing him half his clients and income. But by then, godly financial habits were well-grooved into his management style. He knew from experience how to combat crushing adversity. Sometime later, his business doubled, then doubled again. Some might observe his second revenue doubling and think he was receiving "all at once" overnight success, but it was the result of doing business God's way for many years and having it catch up to him.

This happens a lot. God's financial principles work.

Our creative God customizes a unique path for each of His beloved—and though it often doesn't feel like it in the moment, it's always for our good. The

Lord shows up in wildly creative ways for those who are His. He can meet a need no one knows but you. His mercies are new every morning. God's timing is always just in time.

The best innovation occurs after a setback, not before. It is after you prayerfully devise your best strategy to plow through an obstacle that you put on your brave warrior hat, step into the mess, and strategize new solutions. It is after adversity that these breakthroughs—along with the tumbling effect of wonderful financial growth—occur. Think of the company Zoom. Prior to 2020, few of us knew them. Now they are the standard by which we conduct business. Be brave in adversity. Your time can come.

What about those times when it just doesn't work? I've been there. Those are painful but exquisite lessons in success. Failure can be a wonderful guide.

But sometimes, failure is a rest stop along the ordained path to our dream. When I gave up and sold one of my earlier businesses to a friend for $2,000, I was just three weeks shy of receiving a long-awaited $288,000 contract. Still, I couldn't hold on any longer. Before and after, I felt like a failure, but I wasn't. That particular profit was just not intended by God for me. Oh, I was on my way to success, but the Lord wanted me to pivot in a different direction. I did so only for survival, but I now thank God for protecting me *from* success in order that I might find the greater blessing and success in the ordained work I was "forced" to discover.

Financial Risk of No Bravery after a Failure

The problem with standing still is that everything moves forward—except you. If you label yourself, you limit yourself. Let God do the labeling, the directing, the blessing.

You cannot succeed without bravery, so practice being brave whenever you're standing in even the tiniest gap.

What You Can Do

Do not get emotionally attached to failure. Do not adopt it as your identity. Do not wear it as your label, or embrace it as your brand.

Remember when Tim Tebow rose like a rocket to NFL quarterback greatness and used his worldwide platform to glorify His Savior? Following a game when Tim wore John 3:16 on his *eye black*; the verse was the highest-ranked Google search term over the next twenty-four hours, generating over 90 million searches.[1]

Professional sports can be brutal, and after three short years, Tim was released from the NFL. I lamented that God would allow such a faithful Christian to fail. But Tim refused to wear the false badge of "failure."

The Lord opened a door for him to accept a less prestigious opportunity at minor league baseball, and Tim seized it. But he soon suffered a finger injury that ended his baseball career. Another failure. At the time, many wondered, *Lord, what are you doing?* We could not know that God was using baseball only to expand Tim's platform to an even broader audience.

Tim did not permit failure to compromise his bravery. He knew better than to draw his own finish line before God had finished His plan for Tim's life. Tim Tebow's post-NFL accomplishments are far beyond anything football could offer. God's plan for him was less about saving touchdowns and more about saving lives. Tim is admired and respected around the world for his significant humanitarian,

1 "Tim Tebow." Wikipedia, the Free Encyclopedia. Last modified August 1, 2024. https://en.wikipedia.org/wiki/Tim_Tebow#Denver_Broncos.

ministerial, and philanthropic work. But his success could never have been realized if he hadn't stepped out bravely after failure.

Do not decide where your finish line is. If there is breath in your lungs, you haven't reached it yet.

Give yourself a chance to analyze what went wrong and why. You won't be able to do that if there is self-talk blaring in your head, accusing you of failure. Let the Lord decide where your finish line is. Don't interfere with His success process.

Choose bravery over envy for others whose success arrived sooner than yours. Take every thought captive except those thoughts that lead you forward.

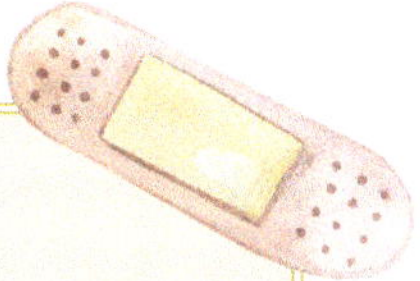

Wound Recovery Checklist

1. Confront your wound. Call it by name.
2. Be alert to triggers that remind you of it. They will be unique to you.
3. Avoid tempting situations. Know your enemy: the enemy of your soul will try to exploit any situation that echoes your negative past.
4. Speak truth to yourself. Affirm your identity in Christ.
5. Ask God to heal you, layer by layer.
6. Make a conscious decision to live life loved. Write it down. Read it daily.
7. Forge ahead with confidence, moving forward, not backward, by taking little steps to live in truth and grace.

Part III

The Winning Ways of the Wealth-Blessed

PUT GOD AT THE CENER

Chapter Nine

YOUR WEALTH-BLESSED MIND: CHOOSE A FINANCIALLY ELEGANT PERSPECTIVE

Why is it that certain wealthy people—wonderful people—are suffering despite all the money in the world while others are satisfied, joyful, and content? How can a wealthy person become happy and wealth-blessed? We can learn a lot by watching the winning ways of those who live a wealth-blessed lifestyle.

And I did:

- The wealth-blessed think and plan differently.
- The wealth-blessed love and spend differently.
- The wealth-blessed interact with God—and with wealth—differently.
- The wealth-blessed express their individual styles and uniqueness differently.

What a revelation it was to me. In the next four chapters, I'm going to show you how they do it. What are their attitudes, emotions, decisions, and lifestyles like? How do they manage...life?

One thing is indisputable: the wealth-blessed know the secrets of contentment. They experience the same hopes, dreams, fear, shame, and anger as we all do. But they know what to do with them.

Mind, Heart, Spirit, and Style

I was surprised to discover an unmistakable connection between financial wellness and the alignment of one's mind, heart, spirit, and style. Until we make the electrifying connection between our money, values, and heartfelt dreams planted by God—until we connect and ignite these disparate elements of mind, heart, spirit, and style—it's unlikely we'll ever find the lasting financial peace and satisfaction we crave, no matter how substantial our wealth.

Some earnest Christians have been busy earning and investing, and they haven't yet focused their *minds* on the future. They haven't considered threats lying in wait, or holy financial opportunities before them. Having attained success in the competitive marketplace, they think they can rest from further planning and still experience financial significance.

Planning is a biblical imperative. Without it, we are less likely to sustain financial security or make a substantial impact. Our future needs and desires, however noble, may go unfunded. What good is the dream of a legacy if our financial life is in shambles?

Some of the most loving Christians I've ever known haven't connected their hearts to their finances. They receive God's wealth with guilt instead of excitement about their opportunity to make a lasting Kingdom impact. They spend joylessly, robotically, in mindless synchronization with their social circle—and wonder why they wrestle with depression.

Some sincere Christians believe they've surrendered their lives to the Lord, but they retain lordship over just one thing: their money. Finances tightly gripped, the subject of money lies just outside the parameters of their otherwise godly lives.

You may be in the first generation of your family to achieve wealth. What a wonderful blessing! You aspire to live a happy, wealth-blessed lifestyle. But what if you were raised in financially difficult circumstances or by someone who managed money unwisely? Despite your sincere desire, you may not know what it *looks like* to synchronize godliness and wealth. How can these coexist? In practical terms, what does this lifestyle look like?

For many of us, all we know about living with wealth is what we read in the news or see on television—which is not the wealth-blessed way—and not the path to lasting financial wellness under God. Without a model, we have no vision. The Bible says that without a vision, the people perish (Proverbs 29:18). I believe their wealth can perish, too.

We need a real-life model of a happy, healthy, responsibly rich way to live under God. So, let's look behind the curtain and uncover the emotions, attitudes, and beliefs that distinguish these interesting, happy, wealthy Christians.

The next four chapters will provide you with God's practical principles for handling and managing His wealth. Adhering to these principles and aligning your mind, heart, spirit, and style with your money will give you peace, contentment, assurance, holiness, and all the joy that goes into being truly wealth-blessed. Now let's see how the wealth blessed do business—with life…

They Tell Their Money Where to Go—and What to Do

Wealth-Blessed Christians are masters, not servants, of the monies that flow through their hands. But how can you lead money if you don't know where you are trying to lead it?

To tell money what to do requires three things:

1. You must know where you want the money to go.
2. You must know what you want the money to do.
3. You must have some money you can order around.

One reason they have money they can order around is because they resisted the urge to spend or squander every precious dollar they worked so hard to earn. The wealth-blessed postpone gratification and eschew grand expenditures. They live underneath their means. They regard earnings as a trust to be handled with care.

Though the wealth-blessed master their money, they do not seek control of it. Rather, they seek to be *under* control—of the Lord. Despite wealth, money is not their god and not their focus.

Since God is not a God of disorder, but of peace, their finances are orderly and meticulously maintained, with a sacred hierarchy of giving, saving, and spending. They are organized, peaceful, and prepared.

They Have a Strong Financial Identity

Their financial identity is strong and fixed on Christ throughout the highs and lows of building and sustaining wealth. Even on those occasions when adverse circumstances threaten wealth, they remain responsibly rich, both in externals, such as giving, and in internals, such as self-talk. With God at the center of their financial identity, they know they'll be all right, despite temporary setbacks. Contrast that to those who wear financial distress as a badge from which they can never escape.

They Know Who Owns It

Wealth-Blessed Christians know they don't own anything. They live in the reality that their lives and all their assets are on the rental plan, at the end of which they will meet the Lord. Since they rent their lives, they can afford to hold the things of this world lightly.

Thankful that God has invited them to carry part of His treasure, they safeguard it wisely, knowing it isn't theirs to keep—but to manage. They think of themselves this way:

They are the ball carriers. But it isn't their ball. They are the King's messengers. But it isn't their message. They are the wealth-bearers. But it isn't their wealth.

Instead, they rightly regard themselves as holding sacred positions. They are trusted executive directors of the King's resources. Squandering is not an option.

They Finesse Financial Disruptions

To finesse requires agility, which takes practice. Athletes practice thousands of hours to develop agility. Spiritual athletes do, too.

The wealth-blessed live their financial lives as if on a grand adventure to tame the temporal man or woman within. They use minor (and major) aggravations and adversities the same way an athlete in training uses increasingly difficult exercises—to refine, strengthen, and empower them to live the holy and wealth-blessed lifestyle they desire.

To finesse requires a calm mindset, which can only exist in a faith-filled environment of trust. When financial setbacks occur, they remain solid. Stable. Not easily shaken. They adapt to financial disruption without losing their financial way.

They are proof we can live remarkably free of financial angst at almost any level.

They Save—All the Time, Every Time

Wealth-Blessed Christians don't save because they're wealthy. They're wealthy because they saved.

"The wise man saves for the future, but the foolish man spends whatever he gets" (Proverbs 21:20, TLB).

In addition to systematic saving, they also allocate a predefined portion of every windfall to savings, as well. This is in stark contrast to those who exempt their windfalls from stewardship and use them only to splurge. Not the wealth-blessed. They give some, save some, and spend some. Little splurges are enough to satisfy them.

They Underspend

These are thoughtful spenders. They could spend rashly if they wished since the funds are there to do so, but rash decisions are not God's way. So, they trade rashness for reasoned, biblically wise decisions. They prioritize where to spend. They are thrifty. They buy less—and smarter. They could afford to be careless about money, but carelessness isn't what got them here. These are big-box store shoppers.

Thrift habits run deep. Thrift helps create and sustain wealth.

When thrift is administered with a mindset surrendered to Kingdom purposes, it lives like thrift on steroids.

"For what will it profit a man if he gains the whole world (wealth, fame, success), but forfeits his soul? Or what will a man give in exchange for his soul?" (Matthew 16:26, AMP).

The wealth-blessed underspend yet they over-enjoy. They know that to over-spend is to curse one's own finances. They are among the happiest people I've ever known.

They Profit

Wealth-Blessed Christians love profit—but they define it differently. As they interact with wealth, they're always seeking to enhance their "inner wealth." In this way, every day becomes profitable.

They enjoy the ride, the process of dealmaking, because they know they are a pipeline. Their fervent belief is, "What comes to me, comes *through* me."

They keep score…but do it differently. Their dealmaking is fascinating to watch. Opportunities and cost savings appear to rain down on them from Heaven.

Sometimes, they pay less—far less. And sometimes, they pay more—far more, such as when God uses them to rain His blessings over another in need…perhaps to help someone keep a job, make a sale, or pay a mortgage. Humbled to be used for God's purposes, they embrace the sacred honor of paying more, knowingly and willingly.

They Act

The wealth-blessed are dreamers. But also, doers.

"Dreaming instead of doing is foolishness, and there is ruin in a flood of empty words" (Ecclesiastes 5:7, TLB).

Admittedly, it feels a whole lot safer to talk about dreams rather than risk embarrassment by attempting them. But, after the wealth-blessed seek counsel and pray, they act on plans and projects. It takes courage to be a doer and not just a talker. But they believe *"All hard work brings a profit, but mere talk leads only to poverty"* (Proverbs 14:23).

How do they muster the courage to act? Because they know…

- The outcome doesn't depend on them.
- If they fail, God will pick them up.
- Success will be measured in many ways beyond the immediate financial outcome.
- As heirs of Jesus Christ, their esteem will be unaffected by the success or failure of any venture they take on.
- The proposed project may be part of God's orchestrated plan, so they can meet a certain person, learn a certain lesson, or become equipped to do a certain something else.

They Work...and Retire

Some people fantasize that once they attain wealth, they won't have to work. The wealth-blessed accept work is God's plan for us despite the impressive size of their balance sheet.

Whether they work at home or in the field, whether serving their children, colleagues, fellow CEOs, or the homeless, whether paid or unpaid for their labor, they give their all because Christ is the real master they serve (Colossians 3:23-24). These are the people we know we can trust even when nobody's looking; for no matter their task—mountainous or mundane—they always work for Christ and not for man.

On the Sabbath, the wealth-blessed shift their mindset and do everything within their power to refrain from working. One fast-food chain is well known for taking that courageous stance. By honoring God's command, Chick-fil-A somehow sells more products in six days than most other fast-food chains sell in seven.

The wealth-blessed retire in varying ways. Some linger in work as long as possible to serve their clients and employ workers. Others retire quickly to move on to the ordained work they feel called to do, work that may pay little, if anything. For the wealth-blessed, post-retirement work is often the most sacrificial and meaningful work of their lives. Their selfless post-retirement acts of service are awe-inspiring.

They Stay Alert

The wealth-blessed stay alert...

...alert to their assets. They heed God's word to "know the state of their flocks," and that without stewardship, money takes off on wings and can fly away (Proverbs 27:23). So, they examine their bank and investment statements, receipts, and credit card statements on a regular basis. One reason they want to protect wealth is to do greater good for God's Kingdom.

...alert to their giving. They monitor progress on their established giving goals. Giving is their highest order of financial rank. Is it any surprise God finds them useful?

...alert to their righteousness before God. They know nothing is as financially treacherous as pride and arrogance. So, they stay sober and alert to any hint of these and other sins in their daily interactions with others. They keep a current account with the Lord, confessing sin immediately. They stay right with God and as safe as they can financially.

Chapter Ten

YOUR WEALTH-BLESSED HEART: CHERISH A HEART-CENTERED APPROACH

The wealth-blessed are heart-centered in their money management. A purpose-driven heart surrendered to Christ is a formidable asset. They awaken their hearts and find a joyful purpose for the funds God flows through their hands.

They Are Content and Satisfied

The wealth-blessed are content and satisfied. Not because they can buy more stuff, but because they don't crave more stuff. In conversation with them, you soon realize how detached they are from money.

How, you wonder, can they be so relaxed and satisfied? Have they been lulled into believing they have more wealth than they have? Not at all.

They're financially relaxed because they spend less than they have. These dear people don't chase after money. Yet, it seems to flow toward them. They are childlike in their delight and appreciation for the smallest things. They express gratitude to the Lord for even the tiniest blessings. These are not the ones with the biggest, grandest houses or the finest cars. They may not own expensive jewelry or fine leather purses. Their shoes may be old. Their purse might be a macrame gift made by a grandchild. They may even fly coach. But their hearts are filled with gratitude and contentment. Simply put, they are easily satisfied.

In contrast, chronically dissatisfied people tend to spend—spend before they save, before they give, before they plan. I've had clients whose annual income was nearly one million dollars, who lived barely on the upside of bankruptcy. It's how dissatisfied individuals often live their lives. But wealth-blessed Christians save and give first, pay their required taxes, and only then do they spend.

Their demeanor and expression are that of gratitude and appreciation. It costs less to satisfy them.

Is contentment a natural result of wealth? No. Contentment is a decision that precedes wealth.

No matter our circumstances, we can choose to be satisfied today, even as we pray for what we'll need tomorrow. In contentment, we become praise-oriented, not crave-oriented. By focusing more on thankfulness and less on what's missing or not perfect in our lives, we steady our emotions and strengthen our wealth.

By guarding our affections, we guard our wealth.

"But godliness actually is a source of great gain when accompanied by contentment (that contentment which comes from a sense of inner confidence based on the sufficiency of God)" (1 Timothy 6:6, AMP).

If we feel chronic discontent, dismissing God's various blessings in our lives because they do not meet our high standards or perfect expectations, we need to stop, think, repent, and give thanks.

They Trust

The wealth-blessed seem trusting. But don't be fooled. Here's their secret: the One they trust is the Lord. This trust allows them to move forward when others are stuck. They're confident to risk a mistake because they know if they make a mistake, it won't mean their whole lives are a mistake. They embrace the Scripture, *"Trust in your money and down you go! Trust in God and flourish as a tree!"* (Proverbs 11:28, TLB).

They Don't Love Money

The wealth-blessed worship God alone, Father, Son, and Holy Spirit, and no other gods before Him. They don't worship money—or anything money can buy. Above all else, they guard their affections against any signs of a growing attachment to money.

Their focus is not on living in the fullness of their bank account, but living in the fullness of their life in Christ.

Money is not their mission, but merely a useful tool. Since they don't love money, they're protected from many financial scams. They have no interest whatsoever in investment schemes or hot financial trends. They're on board with God's admonition regarding the mindset of get-rich-quick. God is a get-rich-slow kind of God.

Shopping is *not* a way of life for the wealth-blessed. They're dispassionate about acquiring new possessions. They feel no desire to impress. Their identity is not

rooted in possessing every new product that comes on the market. They don't need the trappings of wealth—because they are not trapped by wealth.

It's amusing how, sometimes, the wealth-blessed even seem a little financially out of touch. They may not drive the latest model car or use the latest technology. Some fly economy class. They don't need a seat labeling them first class to know that as God's beloved, they are first class. And through Jesus Christ, they hold a prepaid first-class ticket to Heaven.

"Those who love money will never have enough. How meaningless to think that wealth brings true happiness" (Ecclesiastes 5:10, NLT).

How wise of them to guard their affections.

They Don't Hate Money

Wealth-Blessed men and women find no reason to hate money. They're excited by the usefulness of money to serve the Lord, bless His beloveds, and build His church. They're spiritually open and alert to whatever God might want to use regarding money, talent, skill, and every resource on loan to them from the Lord.

They Abhor Debt

The wealth-blessed pay off their homes, drive old cars to avoid making payments on new ones, and pay their credit card bills in full every month. Being debt-free is a lifestyle, an elegant and godly financial rhythm that hums along without the angst of suffering subjugation to loan officers. They're not against the concept of interest—as long as the interest is paid *to* them—not *by* them.

They Fear

Wealth-Blessed Christians have fears, like the rest of us. But they don't fear wealth. They don't think money is a snake that might bite them. Rather, they wisely fear the limitations of the sinful, self-focused human self. They fear…

- Missing what God is directing them to do with their money.
- Accidentally tuning Him out.
- Running out of time to do good.
- Not giving enough. Earning enough. Doing enough.
- Squandering their opportunities.

They fear wasting time, truth, money, abilities, talents, influence, exposure, and above all, wasting the platform God has assigned them through wealth.

Here is a fascinating composite of comments my wealth-blessed clients shared with me over the years about their fears. These reveal the true heart and distinct character of a wealth-blessed person.

I fear not being all He made me to be.

I fear trusting my money instead of the Lord. Or thinking I achieved wealth without Him.

I fear squandering the amazing opportunities He's given me.

I fear becoming selfish and self-centered.

I fear spending on myself the part of my wealth He intends for others.

I fear missing what God is directing. Becoming complacent, tuning Him out.

I fear giving to the wrong church, ministry, or person in need.

I fear becoming too self-sufficient.

I fear laziness. I don't have to work, but I know God wants me to work.

I fear my own lack of faith to give a greater percentage of my income or assets than I'm currently giving. (This comment came from a client who was already giving away 37 percent of pre-tax income and was striving to increase it to 40 percent.)

They Live Financially Loved

When children feel loved by their Father, they don't feel guilty if a blessing comes their way. They don't feel a sneaky need to disguise their pleasure or hide from His presence as if God didn't want them to have that blessing. They realize it is God who provided, approved, and gave this treat to His beloved child.

At times of financial sorrow, they know God loves them and will not abandon them. That He delights in the littlest starts, and when they stumble, He will weave every stumble into a pattern for good. They look beyond themselves to Him for financial provision, so their esteem is never at risk. This gives them more courage to try and to do, to learn and to grow. They trust the Lord to direct their financial steps, and they actively listen for His direction above the din.

They feel more than loved. They feel cradled by the affection and financial provision of their perfect Father.

They Forget

One of the most fascinating attitudes of the wealth-blessed is their focus on the future over the past.

Did they lose money on a project? Oh, yes. Did they try an initiative that didn't work? Yep, that too. Did they fail at a goal? Ha! Don't even ask!

Even so, they don't wallow in self-pity. They don't seethe or simmer in a slow boil over every injustice or unfairness. They take their hits, learn their lessons, and keep their eyes on the winding road ahead.

While others are stuck seething over the unfortunate past, the wealth-blessed tend to press forward into the future, even before the past is resolved. One might say they fail forward.

Their mindset is sweetly sheepish. *"Oh yeah. That didn't go so well. Why don't we try this, instead?"* These delightful people remind me of children. When a child doesn't get the right answer on a math test, they don't spew blame and wrath. They don't declare, "God must not want me to master mathematics." They keep practicing until they get it right.

They Are Joyful and Purposeful

The wealth-blessed believe their role in life is to glorify God in every way and, most decidedly, in their finances. Their financial life is imbued with meaning and purpose. They know they don't own any money. God owns all the money.

They don't believe their wealth is about them. They celebrate their gifts and talents— including the talent to earn money—as a purpose-driven platform for Him. Since they are, as are all of us, uniquely qualified in at least one arena, they use everything—everything—for the glory of God.

They want to be all He made them to be. So, they keep asking questions, listening, learning, and seeking His will.

They play a spiritual "match game," seeking to discern where their assets might minister God's love and provision to someone in need. These big-hearted

Christians are delighted to discover a need they can meet with God's money through their generous, open hands.

What a uniquely ordained life they live. Through them, the following Scripture comes to life: *"For we are His workmanship, created in Christ Jesus for good works, which God prepared beforehand so that we would walk in them"* (Ephesians 2:10, NASB).

They Are Uninterested in Status

Wealth-Blessed Christians appear detached from the spoils of wealth, indifferent to the pulls of status and showiness. Though they can well-afford it, they don't always drive the best car or wear expensive clothes or jewelry. Rat race? No thanks—not for them. They exit any race that pits their self-esteem against others making financial choices. Their money is God's money intended to serve God's purposes.

They are dispassionate to status and prestige and not ensnared by the opinions of others. This is freeing. Sometimes laughingly so.

One client, Brian, who could afford any auto he wanted, or maybe even a whole auto dealership, decided to buy himself a Volkswagen "Bug"—just for the fun of it. He wanted the experience. He drove that car back and forth to his business for a couple of years. Did it matter to him that at valet parking, maybe they thought he was on a tight budget? Not one bit.

"The fear of human opinion disables; trusting in GOD protects you from that" (Proverbs 29:25, MSG).

Wealth-Blessed Christians avoid the snare of worrying about what other people think. Humility is fun for them, and it gives them a chance to learn quickly about another person.

At a stuffy party I attended, someone asked Carrie what she did for a living. Smiling, she shrugged, "Oh, I work in an office." I wondered what job the questioner presumed she had. Carrie did work in an office. She was lead counsel at a law firm.

The craving for status can often rear its ugly, prideful head when it comes to giving. But wealth-blessed Christians enjoy the fun of ignoring status, and they often give anonymously.

They go to great pains to make sure no one finds out they were the ones who provided relief, provided tuition, made it happen, made it work. These spiritual "secret Santas" are used by God all the time to help make life better for His beloveds—and without the neediness to be praised, thank you, anyway!

The wealth-blessed have no need to impress. Their houses may or may not be impressive. Rarely, if ever, have I seen them purchase a house at the top of their financial ability to pay. But to me, the funniest thing is that sometimes, the wealth-blessed fly coach. As one who wangles every loyalty program I can find to maneuver airline upgrades, I find it hilarious to see someone who could buy the entire first-class section of a jet sitting in row 25, crunched next to an oversized stranger in the middle seat.

This doesn't mean that a wealth-blessed Christian never drives a fine car, lives in a fine home, or flies first class. But whatever they do is done independently of what others may think.

They are indifferent to status. They spend on their values.

They live and *spend* for an audience of One. And you and I can, too.

Chapter Eleven

YOUR WEALTH-BLESSED SPIRIT: CULTIVATE SPIRITUAL ALIGNMENT IN WEALTH MANAGEMENT

The wealth-blessed make brave and wise spiritual commitments.

They Start

The wealth-blessed feel free to start all sorts of new projects for one obvious reason: their self-esteem is not built on perfection—it's built on a relationship with a Father they trust. They know if they don't get every little detail right at the start, that's fine—they can modify and tweak their strategy as they go. They trust they will never fall further than their Father's arms can reach.

Unlike frightened others, they're undeterred by fear of failure. Fearless initiators, they're constantly in motion, launching new projects, plans, businesses, careers, and ministries. They explore new hobbies, friendships, and paths. They're not paralyzed by a fear of failure, for they trust God's promise to weave any setback into a pattern for good.

Sometimes, these brave souls don't even know exactly what they are doing in a new start-up and are forced to trust Him moment by moment. This makes the ride even more thrilling for them as they seek to discern and do His will. It's wonderful to watch them in motion.

It would be impossible to count the number of ventures and start-ups of wealth-blessed individuals committed to living in fearless obedience to God and His money. Their bravery is spelled t-r-u-s-t.

...And They Start Over

The uninformed might envision the lives of the wealth-blessed as free from suffering. Unfortunately, not on this planet. Terrible injustices happen to the wealth-blessed, just like they happen to everybody else.

It's astonishing to count the number of wonderful and talented people who've had to start over, often very late in life. These faith-filled people are all around us: they are our neighbors, our colleagues, and our friends.

My client, Cyril, was a well-known, longtime business owner who lived in a grand home. No one knew that during a disastrous financial season that occurred when he was in his seventies, there was a time when he couldn't even afford to replace his broken barbecue grill in that grand home.

People who start over hide in plain sight. You and I can rarely tell from the outside the financial despair that's happening inside their private lives.

Worse, they may have had to start over more than once. But time and again, I've witnessed God's mighty providence in the lives of His beloved as they begin again, even when their loss occurs later in life. This includes my client, Cyril, who persevered in faith and was restored to financial wholeness. Nothing humbles me more than seeing God's beloved transformed from having lost everything…to becoming wealth-blessed again.

They Forgive

The wealth-blessed keep clean and current in their forgiveness. As highly active as they are, it's inevitable that, at some point, someone takes unfair advantage of them. To not block their forward motion—spiritually or financially—they forgive and move on. This doesn't mean they'll do business in the future with one who wronged them, but they do forgive the injuries of the past. And if a wrong was caused by their own imperfect selves, they're quick to ask forgiveness and seek God's forgiveness through Christ.

They Give

The wealth-blessed know generosity is more than the right thing to do. It's the smart thing to do. One of the most brilliant strategies for a wealth-blessed life is to live it generously.

"One person gives freely, yet gains even more; another withholds unduly, but comes to poverty. A generous person will prosper; whoever refreshes others will be refreshed" (Proverbs 11:24-25).

The wealth-blessed give a whole lot more money than we realize. Since they don't talk about what they give, it's harder to study them and learn from them. They're often reluctant to disclose their acts of inspiring and radical generosity because God's Word directs that we'll be rewarded either in Heaven or on earth... but not both. All this silence on the matter makes it difficult for us to learn how to be wealth-blessed.

As one with up-close access, it was humbling to watch their acts of extreme generosity: giving away large assets like boats, RVs, stock holdings, and shares of ownership in commercial real estate. I was privileged to see this over and over again—but only because I was the financial advisor. The wealth-blessed aren't talking. That's why you need to hear these truths from me.

You cannot believe the creativity of these givers. One client wrote a book and dedicated 100 percent of his book royalties to Kingdom causes. Though he served in ministry and lived on a modest income, he and his wife agreed they could manage on the assets they already owned.

Soon, he wrote a second book and a third. He went on to write about a dozen more. It's rare for an author to earn enough income from book royalties to even survive. But the royalties for this generous author totaled an eye-popping one million dollars. Would these books have sold as well had he not dedicated them to the Lord's work? I don't know. What do you think?

They Cater to VIPs

The wealth-blessed cater to those whom God defines as spiritual VIPs. *"Religion that God our Father accepts as pure and faultless is this: to look after orphans and widows in their distress and to keep oneself from being polluted by the world"* (James 1:27).

High on the wealth-blessed VIP list are widows and orphans, the elderly and infirm, the poor and forsaken, and the imprisoned. The wealth-blessed proactively offer their time, talent, treasure—and truth. In certain circumstances, they lend, knowing they may never be repaid. They know their own souls are nourished when they are kind. And their own souls are harmed when they are cruel (Proverbs 11:17). Since God loves widows, orphans, and the poor, the wealth-blessed do, too.

They Listen

Some people envy the wealth-blessed for having God's ear. But it's the reverse.

God has their ear. They're always listening to the Lord and seeking ways to match the instructions from His tongue with the resources in their hands. These highly attentive listeners enjoy matchmaking. They count it a privilege to match God's resources to God's beloveds. Whether the need is expressed by news media or over a shared cup of coffee with a friend, they're always listening and asking the Lord if, in this instance, their giving would help or hinder the Lord's plan.

They listen for God's guidance on how to serve, encourage, or speak. Their prayerful ears are attuned to opportunities to befriend, include, or offer care.

They Refuse to Listen

If any so-called expert tries to convince them to veer from God's clearly written financial instruction, they refuse. However well-meaning, any words spoken to them by a spiritually tone-deaf person bounce off their spiritually well-tuned ears.

If a so-called advisor suggests, for example, that rather than tithing and giving, they should instead put those funds to work to grow and accumulate more wealth, so that they can later write an even bigger check, or if the advisor infers that they are foolish for not leveraging an asset by taking on unnecessary debt, they refuse to listen. Their arms cross, and their ears close. Their spiritual boundaries are firmly fixed. Any words that don't align with God's Word are refused at the door of their soul. Whether it's professional counsel or lies from the enemy or the late-night rantings of their lesser self, the wealth-blessed take every thought captive to the obedience of Christ (2 Corinthians 10:5).

They Are Stubborn

Wealth-Blessed Christians are stubborn about managing wealth God's way—and no other. They know that precisely targeted stubbornness can make them prosper.

So, they are stubborn to give. Stubborn to save. Stubborn to receive counsel before making final decisions. Stubborn to please an audience of One.

Stubbornness protects. Stubbornness prevails.

They Seek Counsel

One of the most endearing—and brilliant—practices of the wealth-blessed is that they seek godly counsel at every turn. This is their secret power.

Whether they're researching a good investment strategy or a reliable roofer, the wealth-blessed listen to professional advice. Because they model sincere respect for people of every status and profession, those whose counsel they seek tend to buy into their cause, whatever it may happen to be, and advocate the best counsel possible.

As an investment advisor, I was often surprised when those with more wealth, education, or business acumen would earnestly seek my professional counsel.

These clients were as well-equipped as I was to manage their investment portfolios. But they knew better than to limit themselves to the preprogrammed loops of their own thinking. They wanted to hear godly financial wisdom from someone *other than themselves* who knew the financial landscape—and knew the Lord. As I spoke, I'd often sense they had one ear tuned to me, the other ear straining toward Heaven to verify confirmation of my counsel.

"Plans fail for lack of counsel but with many advisers they succeed" (Proverbs 15:22).

They Plan

First, they dream. Then, they seek counsel. Then, they plan and strategize, anticipating and detailing how to address potential obstacles. Planning for negatives does not mean they're pessimistic. Planning is not counter to optimism. It's the reverse. They're calm, deliberate, detailed, and forward-thinking.

Planning for the worst affords them permission to be realistic and optimistic at the same time because they are well-prepared. Aside from planning for grander life goals, these are the people who plan for smaller financial irritants they know will arise. They estimate the

useful life of their appliances. They plan years before they replace their automobiles and start saving for them.

They mitigate risk by investing in insurance. And are less likely to be blindsided by the stuff of life because they plan for abstract unknowns they cannot imagine. As a result, when an expenditure catches them unaware, it does not catch them unresourceful.

They Pray

The wealth-blessed pray about money. To ensure their prayers are effective and not contrary to God's will, they study His Word. Despite active schedules, they set aside a quiet time to commune interruption-free with the Lord.

They understand the clear distinction of what prayer is—and is not. They know praying is not the same as worrying, wishing, hoping, positive thinking, or even planning. They don't "waste" their prayers. There's no point asking for money without bothering to read what the Lord has already written about it. If they prayed to win the lottery, knowing God instructs a get-rich-slow mindset, that prayer would be wasted. If they prayed for harm to befall a competitor, so they might take over market share, that prayer would be wasted.

Rather, they pray in alignment with God's financial laws, so their prayers will be heard and fruitful. With access to over 2,000 references to money in Scripture, they soon learn how He wants them to pray.

The effective prayers of the wealth-blessed are for wisdom, favor, grace, the gift of discernment, and for opportunity, effectiveness, fidelity, stamina, self-discipline, and focus, all so that they might glorify Him in their work and receive His financial blessing.

They Forsake Ruin

The Bible is full of wonderful instructions on how to attain, grow, and safeguard wealth. But the wealth-blessed stay alert to the granddaddy of financial threats that might cost them everything: pride. They know nothing is as assured to take them down as pride, because pride is not just idolatry (which God hates), but is the worst form of idolatry: idolatry turned to self. The scriptures regarding pride are terrifying.

Pride isn't about what we *have*, but rather about how we *feel* about what we have. Pride is about smugness of self, superiority over others, and a zealous drive for autonomy—independence from God. Resisting and forsaking financial pride is extremely difficult and requires 24/7 fierce intentionality, because pride is shamelessly used as a lure, as bait by advertisers to manipulate us into buying all sorts of expensive products we do not need and may not even want.

Indulging in financial pride is risky business, like teetering on the edge of a steep, jagged cliff. Many good people have gone over that cliff due to *no other cause* than financial pride.

Pride is a spiritually toxic condition that deadens humility, freezes generosity, and chokes gratitude to the Lord, the True Owner of everything that exists in the world. Pride is a serious offense to God; a spiritual state He does not tolerate for long. *"Pride goes before destruction, a haughty spirit before a fall"* (Proverbs 16:18).

The price of pride is total financial destruction, but secular society seems blind to that fact. In some aspiring social circles, a lifestyle built on pride is a common pursuit among peers. But our societal pressure to impress does not impress God. Pride feeds ego. God wants us to feed the poor.

How do the wealth-blessed manage to destroy their pride before pride destroys their wealth?

- By continually monitoring their financial humility.
- By prayers of surrender of all they possess to the Lord who owns it all anyway.
- By practicing generosity in ways that cause them to have to depend on God—and not relying on their prideful selves.

Sometimes, we're tempted to enter pride by a side door as a heartfelt plea for recognition or honor. Perhaps we've not received the recognition we hunger for and truly deserve. But pride doesn't come before honor. Humility does.

"God opposes the proud, but shows favor to the humble" (1 Peter 5:5b).

"Humble yourselves before the Lord, and he will lift you up." (James 4:10).

What a thrilling experience to be lifted up—not by pretentious ego or treacherous pride, but by God himself. First, humility, then honor. That's God's way. The wealth-blessed know each deliberate step toward humility is a safe step *away* from that deadly financial cliff.

Chapter Twelve

YOUR WEALTH-BLESSED STYLE: CELEBRATE THE GIFT OF YOUR UNIQUENESS

We are each a little peculiar about money, and that's more than okay. Many of my wealth-blessed clients had similar financial means. But their lifestyles couldn't have been more different. I saw it at my desk all the time.

Some chose to buy a second home. Others enjoyed the freedom of renting. Some drove luxury cars. Others bought used cars. One person owned three dresses…and three shopping centers.

You get the idea. The only thing my wealth-blessed clients had in common was they each had their own personal and individual style. They picked their pleasures carefully—and exercised restraint in everything else. Nobody had everything *because God was their treasure.* Their charitable donations confirmed it.

Many fear that if they invite God into their wealth story, their individuality will be compromised, and they'll be squeezed into a cookie-cutter Christian lifestyle.

That's not true. It's the reverse. Embracing a financial lifestyle aligned with our faith is what protects our ability to express our individuality, style, and uniqueness.

Christianity is not a club—it's a body. To function at its best, a body needs lots of very different parts. Since the wealth-blessed are consecrated to Him, God uses their varying and quirky styles to fulfill His purposes. In fact, Scripture tells us not to be conformed to the world around us but to be transformed by the renewing of our minds. For reasons known only to Him, God has designed our *financial* print to be as unique as our fingerprint.

These very different types of wealth-blessed individuals authentically connect with all kinds of different people in this hurting world. God wastes nothing.

They Are Cute

Oh, the curious style of the wealth blessed…

Go ahead. Ask them how they achieved financial success, and they'll often stammer. They seem baffled by their own affluence. Bemused…as if they can't quite figure out how it happened. They shrug. All they were doing was following Scriptural financial guidelines.

They're very knowledgeable about God's financial directives. And sometimes adorably naïve about the financial process.

They appreciate the littlest blessings. They show child-like excitement and genuine happiness over small gifts. Small wonders spawn big delights.

Like all of us, they experience seasons of financial dips and drags. Yet they seem downright disaffected by financial adversity. It's as if somehow they don't realize there is now less money in their account. But they do. For them, financial adversity is an external circumstance, having no power to compromise their core identity, which is always responsibly rich in Christ.

They Are Imperfect with Money

I'm puzzled why people expect superhuman perfection from the wealth-blessed. They're sincere and imperfect, like the rest of us. With Jesus as Lord, they're saved by grace, through faith, not by perfection—not by human standards—so that no one may boast.

Good thing, too. Because the decisions of the wealth-blessed are imperfect.

They start businesses that fail. They buy when they should sell. They zig when they should zag.

They cope with the same temptations, memories, and challenges we all share. Some are working hard to overcome flawed attitudes about spending, saving, or giving. All would define themselves as "works in process."

But because they've woven Christ-centered values into their finances, their mistakes are rarely based on foolish impulse. And less likely to be of a frightening magnitude. When things go sideways, they're resilient about getting up again, because they know God has their back.

They Are Financially Elegant

God's financial laws produce a certain elegance. Dictionary.com describes elegance as "graceful in form or movement."[1]

1 "Meanings & Definitions of English Words." Dictionary.com. Accessed August 22, 2024. https://www.dictionary.com/browse/elegance.

"Gracefully refined and dignified, as in tastes, habits..." The Oxford Dictionary mentions simplicity and neatness.[2] Merriam-Webster describes elegance as "dignified gracefulness or restrained beauty of style."[3]

As people of faith, isn't that how our financial lives should be? Not jagged or disruptive. But simple, refined, and dignified. Isn't there something graceful and elegant about someone who keeps their finances in order? Doesn't it make you wonder why? Doesn't it make you look up?

For an elegant, wealth-blessed individual, financial dignity comes from insisting their bills are paid on time, their spending is under control, and their wealth is purpose-driven, on a mission to serve the Lord. They insist on a financial lifestyle of discipline and order, not chaos. This lifestyle is built before their wealth is built. No wonder they inspire admiration, respect, and sometimes awe.

These are the people we know we can trust with more. Imagine how the Lord feels about that.

They Are at Ease with Money

Wealth-Blessed Christians are at ease around money. Though they have it, they don't seem attached to it. They're casual—even detached.

No passion for it. No pursuit of it.

Their attention, today and every day, is distracted by matters far beyond the temporal. They're aware that here is not Heaven, and they don't try to replicate Heaven by purchasing it.

2 "Elegance Definition." n.d. https://www.oed.com/dictionary/elegance_n?tab=factsheet#5837419.

3 "Definition of ELEGANCE." Merriam-Webster: America's Most Trusted Dictionary. Last modified August 14, 2024. https://www.merriam-webster.com/dictionary/elegance.

For them, nothing needs to come out even, fair, or as planned. It's not a big deal to them if you pick up the check or they do, even if it wasn't their turn. They tend not to turn little things into big things. They're not easily aroused to financial anger. They realize sometimes things work out and sometimes they don't.

They're equally at ease around those who have riches and those who don't. They don't believe that a person who *has* less, *is* less or that a person who *has* more, *is* more. They regard money dispassionately, as a useful tool to serve their families and God's purposes.

They know: *"Your riches won't help you on Judgment Day; only righteousness counts then"* (Proverbs 11:4, TLB).

They Are Interesting

Wealth-Blessed Christians are not boringly self-focused. They're Kingdom-focused, with stories full of excitement about what God is unfolding all around them. Highly invested in Kingdom ministries and initiatives, they have great testimonies about what God is doing in their communities and in the world. That's probably what makes them so interesting to be around.

They Are Governable

Ask any CEO. You have to be manageable to manage. The wealth-blessed often rise to leadership in business and industry. They often describe themselves as "servant leaders," dedicated to helping others rise too. Healed from inner rebellion, they're motivated to be obedient to the King of Kings. They are governable by God and, therefore, highly useful to Him.

They Pay Taxes

I rarely heard much grumbling about taxes from wealth-blessed Christians. I recall lots of eye rolls, to be sure, but the wealth-blessed are compliant and pay what they owe so they can get on with the real business of money—Kingdom business, inspired by God, and not ordered by taxes.

As Jesus instructed, they *"give to Caesar what is Caesar's and to God what is God's"* (Matthew 22:21 NIV). Not one dollar less, nor one dollar more. So, in compliance with God's direction, they shrug, pay their taxes, maybe indulge one last eye roll, and move on.

Though diligent, taxes are not the main factor in their generosity. God says to give to the poor, so if an emergency arises within their circle that is not covered by an official 501c3 ministry, they donate money anyway. They don't depend on questionable worldly strategies that contradict God's financial instructions, such as hanging on to debt to increase tax deductions. *"Let no debt remain outstanding, except the continuing debt to love one another, for whoever loves others has fulfilled the law"* (Romans 13:8 NIV).

Since God says to be in debt to no one, debt offers no appeal.

They Postpone

Postponing gratification is a wealth wisdom strategy not just for the poor but for the wealth-blessed, too. Thanks to the internet, we're all bombarded day and night with shiny trinkets dangled before us, marketed by ingenious methods. But for the wealth-blessed, what delights the eye does not always trigger a purchase. Only foolish people act like that.

They Are Slow Decision-Makers

Wealth-Blessed Christians do not hesitate to demur over some of the most mundane decisions. It drives others crazy, but you cannot pressure these people. You can push, but to no avail. They are any high-powered salesman's worst nightmare, unembarrassed to tell anyone they'll have to pray and sleep on the decision first. They feel no rush whatsoever to jump onto any opportunity that demands an immediate yes. By delaying, they expose sales shenanigans for what they are and save themselves a lot of heartache.

They have predefined criteria for making their buying decisions. And until they're sure the product or opportunity meets that criterion, they pause without embarrassment. Urgency expressed by a sales associate has zero impact on their decision. No sales tactic holds the power to sway their mule-like resistance. They feel no need to prove they can afford anything.

They Have Fun

Wealth-Blessed Christians make money fun. This proves that pursuing holiness over pleasure can still be more fun than managing our finances the world's way.

How can this be? For one thing, they love the excitement of giving to a degree that not all of us are able. They're a different type of "thrill seeker," jumping off cliffs of complacency. In holy trust, they set high goals to serve the Lord and have a fearlessly good time stretching to reach them.

When asked what's their favorite thing about money, you'll hear comments like these:

Giving money away!

Figuring out who to give it to.

Being generous.
Writing big checks.
Being God's instrument, His hands.
Being His boots on the ground.
Connecting people to His compassion, grace, and generosity.
Being a connector of God's people to God's resources.
Being an ambassador.
Serving Him in my unique area.
Living well, with gratitude and contentment, praising God for every little and big thing.
Being used by God as a pipeline from Heaven directly to God's beloved.
Being a secret agent delivering His provision.
Being equipped and empowered to serve without limit.
Having fun using God's money for God's purposes!

They Don't Talk

The wealth-blessed don't talk much about money. Probably because they don't think much about money. *"...For the mouth speaks what the heart is full of"* (Luke 6:45b).

These people are not in love with money. At first glance, one might think the reason is because they already have more than they need. But they never were in love with money, and that's part of why the Lord has blessed them with it.

They don't talk about how much wealth they're giving away. Their left hand doesn't even know the size of the check their right hand has given (Matthew 6:3).

A Tale of Two Lifestyles

Wealth-Foolish	Wealth-Blessed
I'd rather not work at a job. I like my free time.	Free time doesn't pay anything. Why limit my income, choices, and lifestyle? Why hide my talents? Why starve my potential? Why stunt my financial growth? God has given me the direction—and courage—to support myself and my family.
I would never consider homeschooling my children. I prefer the status and money of having a great job.	If I feel called to homeschool, I'm assured my job has the highest status and payout under God: to grow, protect, develop, and train the children He's given me. I will receive a lifetime dividend payout of deepening bonds with them—true status, true riches.
I charge everything to my credit cards. I want what I want now. I don't mind paying four times the price due to interest.	Nope. Indebtedness is enslavement, and why would I pay four times the price? I postpone gratification, and then I outright own what I buy.
I pay interest. Doesn't everybody?	I receive interest.
I'm a financial child.	I'm a responsibly rich grown-up.
I have needs and wants. Others should give money to me.	I have a surplus. I give to others.
I'm financially frustrated.	I'm financially at ease.
Financially, I fake it.	Financially, I'm authentic.
I'm worried and desperate.	I'm confident and calm.

Wealth-Foolish	Wealth-Blessed
I'm angry.	I'm forgiven and forgiving.
I feel financially frightened and alone.	I feel financially safe in the Lord. He's got me.
I hide financial secrets.	I seek financial counsel.
I buy happiness via retail therapy.	I'm immune to sales and marketing schemes.
I'm thankful for the minimum payment options on my credit card.	I hate debt. I'm thankful to pay my credit card balance in full every month.
How can I possibly save?	I save all the time, every time.
I'm quick to leap into opportunities.	I'm slow and methodical in decision-making.
I owe back taxes.	I pay taxes on time and in full.
I'm unhappy with the subject of money.	I feel financial wholeness and happiness at every stage of my wealth development.
I'm grumbling.	I'm prayerful.
Finance is a drag.	Finance is fun.
I receive financial help—by necessity.	I give—by an act of my will.
My financial plans are constantly disrupted.	I finesse financial disruptions.
I feel financially cursed.	I have broken a generational curse.
I'm easily influenced by shady salesmen.	My yes is yes, and my no is no.

Wealth-Foolish	Wealth-Blessed
I keep score of what others have.	I keep counsel of my own faith walk and spiritual growth. I look up, not sideways.
I'm a status seeker.	I'm uninterested in status, except my status before God.
Some find my financial style woeful.	Some find my financial style inspiring, delightful, and unique.
After all, I have my pride!	I have forsaken pride.
I feel financially forsaken.	I feel financially loved.
I hate money.	I don't hate money.
I love money.	I definitely don't love money.
I have a torturous, toxic relationship with money.	I have a healthy, godly relationship with money.
I am anxious.	I am peaceful.
I am discontent.	I am satisfied!

Part IV

Increase Happiness & Live Wealth-Blessed

SEEK HIS PLAN

Chapter Thirteen

GENEROSITY: THE MOTHERLODE OF FINANCIAL HAPPINESS

The Wealth-Blessed Love Adventure

Many interesting adventures are available these days. Thankfully, you can afford most of them. Some adventures involve mountains, oceans, or the heavens. Some focus on height or speed. Some are extremely costly or dangerous. Others require a high fitness level or a specialized expertise. Three exciting components are common to them all. They all require you to…

- Take a risk.
- Reach deep into yourself for strength and moral courage.
- Boldly face an uncertain outcome.

Why do we love to take on these expensive and daring adventures? Because they excite us. Awaken us. Affirm us. Adventure increases our happiness.

But some of us have a hard time finding an adventure we're able to actually participate in. We don't always feel…

Safe enough. Athletic enough. Coordinated enough.

Strong enough. Good enough.

Thankfully, there is one adventure you won't have to miss. If you desire it, you're automatically deemed healthy enough, able enough, young enough, talented enough, skilled enough, and wealthy enough to do it—and to do it well.

GIVING is a world-class adventure. Everybody qualifies. Nobody is ruled out.

Giving is a mountaintop experience, as exhilarating as the highest height and as refreshing as an ocean voyage. The very act of giving is a thrilling departure from the humdrum, a tantalizing dare as you challenge yourself to rise above the tired old grooves of "safe" financial mediocrity. Giving stimulates powerful new self-awareness—and the excitement of God-awareness, too.

Giving is the safest thrill you'll ever experience. You can't fall. You can't fail.

You can't falter. You can't age out.

The only thing in danger…is any residue of selfishness peeking out from your consciousness. Giving doesn't stretch you—it expands you. It makes a small life feel bigger—and a big life feel revitalized. It widens opportunities, amplifies influence, and unlocks access to new interests, relationships, and experiences.

Like all adventures, generosity feels scary at first. Signing a big check can feel a little like skydiving—a financial freefall into you-don't-know-where, especially if it's the largest check you've ever written. But then suddenly, a parachute opens. You didn't open it. God did.

What a thrill when the One who owns it all, catches you. The proud Father is pleased with His generous child for using His wealth the way He decreed. Affirmed and content, you experience financial wellness as never before. You've now proven to yourself that you really do have enough to share grandly. Whether you're giving shares of income, stock, or equity ownership in a commercial enterprise, you experience an overwhelming wave of financial happiness. A surge of wellness. You'll soon see.

Generosity will feed your need for thrill. It reawakens every cell in your body. The bigger the check, the bigger the thrill. The bigger the stretch, the bigger the rush.

My brother is a runner. He'll sometimes run six miles. He says he doesn't do it for physical health as much as for mental health. Running relieves stress and, after a few miles, creates a "runner's high." I do not run. But I don't need to run. A "runner's high" is *nothing* compared to a giver's high.

Three False Beliefs That Block People from Giving

In working with clients over the years, I encountered three common misbeliefs that kept good-hearted Christians from experiencing the joy and thrill of generosity. These misbeliefs close the doorway to financial adventure and happiness, making their world smaller and duller.

1. "Our money belongs to us."
2. "There won't be enough."
3. "Giving is optional."

Let's examine these defective beliefs that close us off from God's fullest blessing.

1. "Our money belongs to us."

Actually, it doesn't.

"The earth is the LORD's, and everything in it, the world, and all who live in it" (Psalm 24:1). Everything we possess, in reality, belongs to God. We own nothing. He owns everything. All of it, including our very lives, are on loan to us.

Even our ability to earn wealth has come from God. *"But remember the LORD your God, for it is he who gives you the ability to produce wealth, and so confirms his covenant, which he swore to your ancestors, as it is today"* (Deuteronomy 8:18).

Why did He allow you to produce wealth? To fulfill His covenant. To complete His purposes.

False: ~~*"Our money belongs to us."*~~
True: *"It all belongs to God."*

2. "There won't be enough."

This is a sincere fear that looks ahead with worry to the state of your business enterprise, your past investment mishaps, worldwide geopolitical conditions, or the current economy—without also factoring in God's economy. God's intention is not to make us financially strapped, but to make us financially mature and wise adults trained and equipped to manage His wealth.

He has overloaded Scripture with detailed instructions on growing and managing wealth and has kindly and specifically warned us about what shuts it down. It turns out it is more dangerous not to give than to give—for if we withhold from Him what God does not intend to be ours, there will never be enough.

"One person gives freely, yet gains even more; another withholds unduly, but comes to poverty" (Proverbs 11:24).

False: ~~*"There won't be enough."*~~
True: *"If we obey God with our giving, there will always be enough."*

3. "Giving is optional."

This is a defective belief that puts us at grave financial risk. In point of fact, giving is a requirement, a nonnegotiable precondition for everyone who receives God's money into their households. The moment we understand this, most of us change our giving habits immediately. Who would want to risk keeping even a few dollars the Lord did not ordain to stay in our hands?

"Whoever shuts their ears to the cry of the poor will also cry out and not be answered" (Proverbs 21:13).

False: ~~*"Giving is optional."*~~
True: *"Giving is explicitly required by God."*

Six Practices for Growing Happiness

For over twenty-five years, I had the rare privilege of observing, at close, unfiltered range, the undeniably increasing happiness of generous givers. These givers were regular people of all income levels. Their lives were not free of problems. Yet they were plugged into an inner spring of perpetual wellness, deeply rooted and not dependent on shifting circumstances. Wellness flowed from their core in dynamic fashion and seemed to sweep away worry and financial concerns—even on those occasions when I, as a professional, voiced concern.

But the pattern was undeniable: even former "non-givers" or "low-givers," who later became generous givers, sometimes late in life, seemed to experience a dramatic upward tilt in temperament, outlook, and overall sense of wellness. At the time, it amazed me. I longed to experience this inner wellness myself. Generous givers didn't have to chase happiness—happiness chased them. I observed this in all generous givers. I watched them grow more confident, peaceful, cheerful, faith-driven, interesting, popular, and connected to others.

Givers Grow More Confident

Those who became generous givers exuded a new air of confidence. I observed this in givers at every financial level—rich, poor, and middle-class. Generous giving generated an esteem-building sense of power, capability, and affluence. This caught my attention because, mathematically, when one gives more, one keeps less. Yet generous givers exuded unmistakable confidence in their circumstances and their ability to manage their lives.

Givers Grow More Peaceful

It might surprise you that financial anxiety is a common malady, even among the wealthy. As a professional, I was frustrated when clients with sizable assets could not let themselves feel safe. They struggled to relax or enjoy family time. Vacations were put off or compromised just to quiet the beating drum of anxiety. These dear clients were accomplished in only two activities: working and fretting.

Financial worry is costly. It ruins sleep, hijacks joy, and empties the fun out of family time. But once these non-givers became generous givers, they seemed to... relax. A new trust replaced that anxious place within. Until they learned to give generously, these dear clients never felt safe. But the sacred act of giving somehow instilled a peaceful, trusting heart and mind.

Givers seemed surer of the future and less uncertain about outcomes. Less dependent on shifting circumstances and more plugged into an unexplainable spring of hope.

I watched in wonder. Giving is truly Rx for the anxious financial soul.

Givers Grow More Cheerful

My professional responsibility was only to assess the financial implications of my clients' choices. I was not on the lookout for changes in their basic temperaments. But I repeatedly witnessed, sometimes in near disbelief, a formerly negative, pessimistic, dismal client gradually morph into a financially cheerful type.

Those who dared dip their financial toes into the water of generous giving had good reason for new cheer. By giving, they were fitting snugly into God's strong economy, and no longer dependent on the world's shaky economy. They had a valid new reason to trust that blessings would open up for them. They were aware there might be some heavenly pruning ahead, yet they were optimistically expectant about what God would do in their financial lives now that He was the One in charge.

Givers Grow More Interesting and Popular

This aspect of happiness caught me by surprise. Sure, when we give, we become holier...but can we become more interesting and popular? Still, I saw it for myself: the answer is a wholehearted yes.

Jesus taught in Luke 6:45 that our mouth speaks from the overflow of our hearts. We tend to talk about, think about, ask about, and give our time to whatever is on our heart.

When our hearts are invested in ourselves, our conversation follows. We soon realize with dismay that other people do not find us nearly as interesting as we do. In fact, the more we talk about ourselves, the more others pull away.

Generous givers are naturally interested—and literally invested—in the outcomes of their giving. When we invest in something outside ourselves, our thoughts, dreams, and conversations become far more interesting.

My husband became aware of a local after-school tutoring ministry for at-risk youth, which reminded him of his childhood. He gave them several financial gifts. Then, he decided to attend one of their events. He loved their program and found himself invested—emotionally now, and not just financially—in the ministry's success. He wanted to give more of himself to make the program all it could be.

Jesus explained it this way, *"For where your treasure is, there your heart will be also"* (Luke 12:34). Eventually, my husband was asked to serve on their Board of Directors. Today, he is its president.

It's just plain fun to be around givers. It's interesting to be with them and talk with them. They seem lit from within by a purpose and passion outside themselves. No wonder they're so popular.

Givers Grow More Faith-Driven

My clientele represented every faith level imaginable, from atheistic to those in full-time ministry. No matter where they began—low giving or no giving—after they began to practice generosity, the trajectory of their faith took an upward turn. Giving somehow joined their hearts to God's own heart. It was as if with one shared heart, they began to see their lives through His holy perspective.

Givers Grow More Connected to Others

Those who began to give generously became more connected to others. These close connections and newly formed alliances positively impacted their emotional wellness—and sometimes their businesses, too. Generous giving ushered in new relationships, fresh opportunities, and interesting engagements and activities of all kinds, including social, faith, and business. Fellow givers within a church or ministry initiative became newfound friends. Former loneliness was transformed into a new fullness of life.

Could giving be a cure for loneliness? The answer, I believe, is yes.

It's Not Too Late

If you haven't yet experienced the thrilling adventure of generosity—nor received the motherlode of financial happiness known to accompany it—it's not too late to start. Today is a new day. Maybe God is doing *"a new thing in you"* (Isaiah 43:19). Some of my clients took their first steps of generosity when they were well into their seventies.

Why does He want you to give? Maybe He wants to enlarge your world.

The honor of being chosen to carry money from God's hand to God's beloved is one of the highest honors on earth. God owns it all, so you never need to ask how much you should give.

Instead, just ask how much of His money you may keep.

Chapter Fourteen

WHY GOOD PEOPLE SOMETIMES LOSE EVERYTHING—AND WHY YOU DON'T HAVE TO

One aspect of wealth most enjoyed by my clients was the freedom to express themselves. Wealth provided almost unlimited choices about how and where to spend and invest. The possibilities were nearly endless when considering where to vacation, which car to drive, and which house—or houses—to buy.

Early in my career, I felt sad that those of us who didn't possess wealth were limited from fully exercising our freedom of expression. But then I learned the dark side of freedom: that wealth does not assure us freedom at all. Money can imprison us, chain us, ruin our relationships, and destroy our lives. The very financial circumstance that kept those without wealth from acting on every little impulse also provided them a steady hedge of protection against disastrous buying decisions, unrecoverable mistakes, and needless heartaches.

I cringed when I realized that my wealthy clients' so-called freedom of expression put them more at risk, for they had no such hedge of protection in place. There is a dark and serious flip side to all that financial freedom.

Wealth: Blessing or Curse?

My wealthy clients had the means to buy, do, or possess almost anything they wanted. And that very freedom was their greatest risk. Wealth beckoned them to speed and spend down life's highway in the fast lane, with financial glee and abandon, and no "financial police" in sight to flash blue lights and stop or slow them down. Regrettably, some of them crashed—and crashed hard.

Thankfully, my wealth-blessed clients lived differently, spent differently, and enjoyed a different outcome. By having invited God into their wealth story and having asked to be part of His, they operated on a higher plane than wealthy others, gliding along at perfect speed on a different kind of highway—a level one (Proverbs 15:19.) Oh, they enjoyed many freedoms, too, but with a significant hedge of extra protection against *unnecessary* disaster and heartache.

What was their secret? From where did they acquire this essential armor that covered their wealth, happiness, and life? How did they keep their financial vehicles on the road?

Guardrails. If you have wealth, you need guardrails, too.

My wealth-blessed clients were well aware that their biggest threat of financial devastation would come not from outside them—not from other people, circumstances, or externals—but from inside them, from the impulses, choices, attitudes, and decisions they were free to make from day-to-day about who they would be, how they would respond to their cravings and wants, how they would do business, and how they would engage in financial relationship—with themselves, others, and God.

Where did these wise, wealth-blessed persons find the guardrails that allowed them to freely pursue God-inspired dreams with speed and intensity yet keep within His holy guidelines? There is only one safe place to find the guardrails we need to keep ourselves from crashing into accidental poverty. It's the Bible.

The Bible is the land of plenty for anyone looking for financial advice. Wealth-sustaining guardrails are plentiful throughout Scripture. Anyone who thinks the Bible doesn't teach us how to earn and sustain wealth has never read it. The Bible is, as mentioned before, loaded with over 2,000 teachings on every facet of wealth management. If you want to receive all God has financially ordained for you, you really should read His Book.

Many of His financial teachings are encouraging and offer hope about how to grow, give, and grant a financial legacy.

Many other teachings express crucial warnings about the large number of significant risks faced by the wealthy every single day.

Below, you'll find forty scriptural guardrails based on common and repeating financial errors—and resulting sorrows—I saw throughout my career. You and I need these guardrails to help keep safe all that we've worked so hard to gain. Our guardrails will cross nine financial lanes:

- Overt dangers
- Counsel and discipline
- Planning, saving, and knowing
- Working and resting

- Pride
- Generosity
- Business transactions
- Control
- Profit

I've chosen most of these guardrails from the book of Proverbs, a treasure trove of financial wisdom. If you want to build and broaden the indirect behaviors that foster a wealth-blessed life, again, I suggest you read Proverbs every day. These will help safeguard you from catastrophic danger and financial heartache. They might even prevent you from losing everything.

Forty Guardrails To Keep You From Losing Everything

On Overt Dangers

1. Watch for prowlers

"Be alert and of sober mind. Your enemy the devil prowls around like a roaring lion looking for someone to devour" (1 Peter 5:8).

2. Don't plunge into ruin

"Those who want to get rich fall into temptation and a trap and into many foolish and harmful desires that plunge people into ruin and destruction. For the love of money is a root of all kinds of evil. Some people, eager for money, have wandered from the faith and pierced themselves with many griefs" (1 Timothy 6:9-11).

3. Act justly—or reap calamity

"Whoever sows injustice reaps calamity, and the rod they wield in fury will be broken" (Proverbs 22:8).

4. Take cover! Quick!

"The prudent see danger and take refuge, but the simple keep going and pay the penalty" (Proverbs 22:3).

On Counsel and Discipline

5. Seek counsel

"Plans fail for lack of counsel, but with many advisers they succeed" (Proverbs 15:22).

"The way of fools seems right to them, the wise listen to advice" (Proverbs 12:15).

6. Discipline or poverty? Pick one!

"Whoever disregards discipline comes to poverty and shame, but whoever heeds correction is honored" (Proverbs 13:18).

7. Promise nothing too quickly

"It is a trap to dedicate something rashly and only later to consider one's vows" (Proverbs 20:25).

8. Be careful in relationships

"Walk with the wise and become wise, for a companion of fools suffers harm" (Proverbs 13:20).

"Do not make friends with a hot-tempered person, do not associate with one easily angered, or you may learn their ways and get yourself ensnared" (Proverbs 22:24-25).

"The righteous choose their friends carefully, but the way of the wicked leads them astray" (Proverbs 12:26).

9. Don't be entrapped

"Fear of man will prove to be a snare, but whoever trusts in the LORD is kept safe" (Proverbs 29:25).

10. Hold tight!

"Hold on to instruction, do not let it go; guard it well, for it is your life" (Proverbs 4:13).

11. Choose "Wisdom Wealth"

"Choose my instruction instead of silver, knowledge rather than choice gold, for wisdom is more precious than rubies, and nothing you desire can compare with her" (Proverbs 8:10-11).

12. No cosigning!

"Do not be one who shakes hands in pledge or puts up security for debts; If you lack the means to pay, your very bed will be snatched from under you" (Proverbs 22:26-27).

"My son, if you have put up security for your neighbor, if you have shaken hands in pledge for a stranger, you have been trapped by what you said, ensnared by the words of your mouth. So do this, my son, to free yourself, since you have fallen into your neighbor's hands: Go—to the point of exhaustion—and give your neighbor no rest! Allow no sleep to your eyes, no slumber to your eyelids. Free yourself, like a gazelle from the hand of the hunter, like a bird from the snare of the fowler" (Proverbs 6:1-5).

On Planning, Saving, Knowing

13. Plan and save for the future

"The plans of the diligent lead to profit as surely as haste leads to poverty" (Proverbs 21:5).

"There is precious treasure and oil in the house of the wise (who prepare for the future), But a short-sighted and foolish man swallows it up and wastes it" (Proverbs 21:20, AMP).

14. Know what you have

"Be sure to know the state of your flocks, and pay close attention to your herds; for riches are not forever, nor does a crown endure to every generation" (Proverbs 27:23-24).

15. Diversify your assets

"Invest in seven ventures, yes, in eight; you do not know what disaster may come upon the land" (Ecclesiastes 11:2).

16. Why all the borrowing? Stop it!

"...the borrower is a slave to the lender" (Proverbs 22:7b).

"Let no debt remain outstanding, except the continuing debt to love one another, for whoever loves others has fulfilled the law" (Romans 13:8).

On Working and Resting

17. Stop talking, start doing

"All hard work brings a profit, but mere talk leads only to poverty" (Proverbs 14:23).

18. Don't play so much

"Whoever loves pleasure will become poor; whoever loves wine and olive oil will never be rich" (Proverbs 21:17).

19. Plow instead!

"Sluggards do not plow in season; so at harvest time they look but find nothing" (Proverbs 20:4).

20. Don't work so much

"Do not wear yourself out to get rich; do not trust your own cleverness. Cast but a glance at riches, and they are gone, for they will surely sprout wings and fly off to the sky like an eagle" (Proverbs 23:4-5).

"Unless the LORD builds the house, the builders labor in vain. Unless the LORD watches over the city, the guards stand watch in vain. In vain you rise early and stay up late, toiling for food to eat—for he grants sleep to those he loves" (Psalm 127:1-2).

21. A wake-up call for the sleepyhead

"A little sleep, a little slumber, a little folding of the hands to rest—and poverty will come on you like a thief and scarcity like an armed man" (Proverbs 24:33-34).

On Pride

22. Save your house

"The Lord tears down the house of the proud…" (Proverbs 15:25a).

23. Don't trust this!

"Those who trust in their riches will fall, but the righteous will thrive like a green leaf" (Proverbs 11:28).

24. Crime and punishment

"The LORD detests all the proud of heart. Be sure of this: They will not go unpunished" (Proverbs 16:5).

25. Beware seven detestables

"There are six things the LORD hates, seven that are detestable to him:
haughty eyes,
a lying tongue,
hands that shed innocent blood,
a heart that devises wicked schemes,
feet that are quick to rush into evil,
a false witness who pours out lies
and a person who stirs up conflict in the community"
(Proverbs 6:16-19).

26. Escape disgrace

"When pride comes, then comes disgrace, but with humility comes wisdom" (Proverbs 11:2).

"Pride goes before destruction, a haughty spirit before a fall" (Proverbs 16:18).

On Generosity

27. Don't be stingy

"The stingy are eager to get rich and are unaware that poverty awaits them" (Proverbs 28:22).

28. Give more, gain more

"One person gives freely, yet gains even more; another withholds unduly, but comes to poverty" (Proverbs 11:24).

29. Keep your eyes and ears open

"Those who give to the poor will lack nothing, but those who close their eyes to them receive many curses" (Proverbs 28:27).

"Whoever shuts their ears to the cry of the poor will also cry out and not be answered" (Proverbs 21:13).

On Business Transactions

30. Tell the truth!

"A fortune made by a lying tongue is a fleeting vapor and a deadly snare" (Proverbs 21:6).

31. Protect your reputation

"A good name is more desirable than great riches; to be esteemed is better than silver or gold" (Proverbs 22:1).

32. Pay fairly

"Whoever increases wealth by taking interest or profit from the poor amasses it for another, who will be kind to the poor" (Proverbs 28:8).

"One who oppresses the poor to increase his wealth and one who gives gifts to the rich—both come to poverty" (Proverbs 22:16).

33. Profit honestly

"Differing weights and differing measures—the LORD detests them both" (Proverbs 20:10).

"Dishonest money dwindles away, but whoever gathers money little by little makes it grow" (Proverbs 13:11).

On Control

34. Control yourself

"Like a city whose walls are broken through is a person who lacks self-control" (Proverbs 25:28).

35. Guard your tongue

"Those who guard their lips preserve their lives, but those who speak rashly will come to ruin" (Proverbs 13:3).

"The tongue has the power of life and death..." (Proverbs 18:21a).

"Those who guard their mouths and their tongues keep themselves from calamity" (Proverbs 21:23).

36. Don't gloat

"Whoever mocks the poor shows contempt for their Maker; whoever gloats over disaster will not go unpunished" (Proverbs 17:5).

"He mocks proud mockers but shows favor to the humble and oppressed" (Proverbs 3:34).

37. Guard your affections

"Above all else, guard your heart, for everything you do flows from it" (Proverbs 4:23).

38. Guard your path

"In the paths of the wicked are snares and pitfalls, but those who would preserve their life stay far from them" (Proverbs 22:5).

39. Who's the boss?

"So if you have not been trustworthy in handling worldly wealth, who will trust you with true riches?" (Luke 16:11).

On Profit

40. Be wealth-blessed

"Blessed are those who find wisdom, those who gain understanding, for she is more profitable than silver and yields better returns than gold. She is more precious than rubies; nothing you desire can compare with her. Long life is in her right hand; in her left hand are riches and honor. Her ways are pleasant ways, and all her paths are peace. She is a tree of life to those who take hold of her; those who hold her fast will be blessed" (Proverbs 3:13-18).

Chapter Fifteen

FORGET WHAT LIES BEHIND, AND REACH FORWARD TO WHAT LIES AHEAD...

No matter your financial history, you can be emotionally healed, spiritually redeemed, and financially restored to wellness. God can redeem even the hardest financial circumstances. It's never too late to create a life of spiritual and financial significance. You haven't run out of time, so don't run out of faith.

Wealth-Blessed Success Stories

Meet four wealth-blessed individuals who faced life-crushing circumstances and financial decimation, and who overcame seemingly insurmountable odds. Some names and details have been changed for privacy, but make no mistake—these are real people, real stories, and real outcomes.

Anna suffered complete and dangerous burnout and had to walk away from a corporate career that had taken twenty years to build.

Barney made one single mistake that virtually bankrupted him.

Harry was the innocent victim of a corporate injustice that cost him his business.

Guy lost everything due to a no-fault personal circumstance.

All four used the tools in their wealth-blessed tool chests to overcome devastating personal and financial circumstances.

Anna's Stellar Success

Anna was gifted with an abundance of brains and talent that perfectly positioned her for the high status and income of her corporate career. Raised in a success-driven household of faith and provided with an impressive education, it was no surprise to anyone when she went on to attain a C-suite pinnacle in a Fortune 500 company. Everybody cheered her stellar rise to corporate success.

But beneath the accolades and applause, Anna felt unhappy, empty, and disheartened. She found it exhausting to pretend to herself that her work mattered. *"Is this all there is to my life?"* She sensed God had something more for her—and wanted something more *from* her. Anna wrestled against the relentless, gentle whispers of the Holy Spirit. How much money is enough? How much status is enough? *"Yes, Lord,"* she protested, *"but don't You appreciate how hard I've worked to get to this position?"*

After months of maddening restlessness, she bravely took a one-year sabbatical from her successful post to focus on God's direction for her future. For this talented overachiever, it would be the first time in her life that Anna had no goal or plan in mind except to listen to—or silence—the Lord's leading and try to find meaning in her life.

God quickly opened doors, and she was introduced to new, dynamic people and interesting local ministries. She volunteered her significant skills, forged new friendships, and formed alliances. Many in her new circle of relationships began to seek her counsel and depend on her brilliant abilities. They invited her to serve on ministry boards, where she applied her talents and made a real difference.

That pivotal year ignited Anna's flame for radical generosity. She was fueled with a new desire to simplify her life so she could spend more of God's wealth for God's purposes—not hers. Something inside her, long stilled by hopelessness, reawakened.

Fast-forward ten years. Today, Anna is the president of a national ministry. Her life is joyful. Her countenance radiates beauty and purpose. She lives simply, but elegantly. Anna is a wealth-blessed success story.

Barney's Big Blunder

Barney was a good man known for financial prudence. Still, like all of us, he was capable of making a drastic mistake. When he was presented with a "can't miss" investment opportunity, *just this once,* he ignored the essential guardrail of seeking counsel. Regrettably, he signed a contract for a large and terrible investment in an undiversified hard asset of commercial real estate. Most of his financial "eggs" went into that unfortunate asset, which seemed to him, on paper, a sure thing. But the situation fell apart, and he lost his wealth—all of it.

Well into his seventies, Barney had been ready to wind down his business. Now, there seemed no hope, but he doggedly refused to give in to pessimism or defeat. After asking the Lord to forgive his error, a flicker of hope renewed. He continued working, praying, trusting, and closely following God's financial direction. Though it appeared impossible on paper, unexplainable blessings began to restore him to wholeness. By the end of his very long life, his wife was left with sufficient funds to live the rest of her days in financial dignity.

Harry's Heavenly Courage

When in his sixties, Harry, an exemplary Christian and spectacular human being, lost everything, including his business, due to nothing other than the unscrupulous dealing of a corporation he represented. His situation seemed hopeless, even to me as his advisor, because Harry had lost not only all his assets, but also his ability to earn an income. Unthinkable financial devastation.

Still, Harry's faith in Christ helped him hold his head high above the financial fray. Heavenly courage ruled his mind and his mood. What a witness he was to me and to many! With no money, he literally started over, as someone would do in their twenties or thirties. By God's grace, his former clients found him in his newly formed company and location. Over a period of years, the Lord restored all that the wrongdoers had taken.

Those were hardworking years but full of excitement and an outpouring of God's glory. Week after week, Harry experienced a heavenly downpour of grace, miracles, and favor as never before. It was a beautiful thing to watch.

Still happily working, he's a renowned success story, a hometown hero, beloved by all. He's long since forgiven his wrongdoers. I

recently attended a celebration honoring Harry's career. His face was radiant, with no shadow of bitterness. Presently in his eighties, he looks sixteen years younger.

Guy's True Grit

And then there's Guy, who lost all his wealth in his mid-fifties due to an impossible personal circumstance. Everything was taken from him except a modest business—and a monstrous debt he could never repay. Despite the panicky plea by his accountant, Guy knew that for him bankruptcy was not an option.

During his first tenuous months starting over, a shocking and dreadful corporate product change split his revenue stream in half—permanently. But with faith, grit, and the cool-headedness one can only maintain through an unwavering faith in his Lord, he restored all that was lost. I know Guy's story even more intimately because, in the midst of his crisis, I married him.

For these and other faith-driven clients too numerous to name, restoration was not fast, easy, or painless, but the spiritual exhilaration and joy they experienced along the way were profound. And note the most important element of the timeline in these true stories: Anna, Barney, Harry, and Guy were wealth-blessed *before* they reached their happy endings.

God has a spiritual purpose for the wealth that flows through us in various seasons, no matter how large or small that flow may be. The abundance He seeks for us must start spiritually, on the inside, before it can hope to overflow to the outside.

And the overflow for Barney, Harry, and Guy?

Oh yes. They got it all back—*all of it.*

The Net Worth of the Wealth-Blessed

The wealth-blessed have mastered the elegant art of stewarding God's money through seasons of poverty, possibility, and plenty. As we peel back the layers of complicated circumstances encountered by people of faith, a picture emerges of a spiritually significant financial life we all dream of living. No matter what the world throws at you, spiritual financial significance is attainable—for you and for all of us—at nearly any income level.

The real-life stories of Anna, Barney, Harry, and Guy span a wide range of income, assets, and lifestyles. But wealth-blessed is not a number—it's a relationship with God and with wealth.

The Wealth-Blessed Financial Statement

If God issued wealth-blessed financial statements, one thing would stand out: it would be the only financial statement ever produced with no numbers on its pages. How can that be? Because being wealth-blessed is not a statement of net worth—it's a statement of net *trust*—in God.

A wealth-blessed profit and loss statement highlights the spiritual profit of a Christ-centered focus in the profit column, and the consecrated relinquishment of fruitless self-focus in the loss column. What a beautiful P&L.

A wealth-blessed balance sheet lists the priceless asset of contentment in Christ. Then, finally, in the column totaling the equity of our balance sheet, we see a number. We look at the figure quizzically. What is that? Then, we feel hushed by God's whisper. It's the total amount of money we've distributed to Kingdom causes over our lifetime.

The Restlessness of the Wealth-Blessed

If you feel restless, guess what? God may be the author of your discontent.

Perhaps He's equipped you with an ability, thus far untapped, and He wants to insert you into a new and significant financial role. It's possible that the God who loves you is nudging you out of your cozy "wealth nest."

Or your restlessness may be about something else. You may be in financial combat with a real adversary. The enemy of your soul and mine is on a 24/7 mission to thwart your opportunity to live a wealth-blessed life. Financial opposition surrounds you. Some may still be buried within you. But you're ready. You have the tools. It's time to take a stand.

Just as you wouldn't invite a burglar into your home to steal your belongings, do not allow a financial villain to steal your spiritual joy. Confront your opposition. Take decisive action by using all the tools in your tool chest:

- Confront the lies that cause you to create financial sabotage (Chapter 2).
- Resolve your conflicts about wealth and ambition by going to God's Word (Chapter 3).
- Follow a proven wealth map to financial strength and wellness (Chapter 4).
- Ask for and receive God's financial therapy for your financial wounds (Chapter 5).
- Offer your past financial hurts to God's light and healing truth (Chapter 6).
- Release your present distress to His care (Chapter 7).
- Reset your financial forecast (Chapter 8).

Study and model the winning ways of the wealth-blessed as they:

- Choose a life of financial elegance (Chapter 9).
- Cherish a heart-centered approach to money (Chapter 10).
- Cultivate spiritual alignment of their wealth management (Chapter 11).
- Celebrate the gift of their own unique financial style (Chapter 12).
- Greatly expand financial and spiritual happiness via generosity (Chapter 13).

Finally, safeguard your wealth by establishing protective guardrails (Chapter 14).

Writing Your Wealth-Blessed Success Story

I don't know God's highest and best will for you. But then...you don't know either.

We can't know His precise plan for our financial lives, and we won't know until we manage our finances His way, not ours. Life is bumpy here on planet Earth, so I can't promise you'll be wealthy or avoid new mistakes. You might even do everything right and never increase the size of your wealth—if that's His will for you. We can never receive more than God has ordained for us. But we can expect to be entrusted with less—if we squander stewardship opportunities.

Your wealth may feel like a runaway train, taking you where you don't want to go. You may feel as if you're trapped in a dark tunnel with no light in sight. Your burnout may be at dangerous levels, your finances about to implode, and you cannot breathe. You may have been served with a judgment—or divorce papers. Nobody even knows about your impending financial debacle.

God knows. If invited, He's ready to step in and help you. Our sovereign God is equipped to deliver the miraculous turnaround you seek. But first, you must seek Him:

Seek Him above money, status, or any other thing you want. Seek *His* deliverance above *financial* deliverance. Seek restoration with Him above restoration of wealth—and relationships. Seek His sovereignty above yours in your business and your personal life.

He can take you through your mess and get you safely to the other side.

He can make life feel worth living again. Turn to Him. Do it now.

We don't know what God will do. We know only what God can do.

His ways are not our ways. But do try. Not for wealth's sake. For Kingdom's sake.

Let go of the unsatisfying frustration and despair that lies behind you. Move toward a beautiful, wealth-blessed way of living. When you commit to using wealth to glorify God, here's how your life will begin to feel:

Satisfying. Simple. Significant.

Peaceful. Purposeful. Elegant.

This is how the wealth-blessed live. So, whether you're starting up, starting over, or finishing well…Invite God into your wealth story. Ask to be part of His.

Close the gaps, heal the hurts, and put God at the center of your finances. You, too, can live a wealth-blessed life.

I can't wait to hear your testimony.

Acknowledgments and Thanks

To the great Lori Roeleveld, my writing and publishing coach, you've steered, shepherded, and saved me from many missteps. The depth of your knowledge and wisdom, the height of your holiness and integrity, and the length of your publishing experience are the winning combination I needed to reach my finish line.

To my publisher, Victoria Duerstock, Michelle Medlock Adams, and all the editors, designers, and team at End Game Press, from the moment I first saw your gorgeous books, I hoped my publisher would be you.

To Guy, the one true love of my life, my handsome prince, for sacrificing many evenings of our snuggle time so I might fulfill my mission.

To the Lord, thank you, Father, for plucking me out of life's refuse and planting me squarely into your family of faith (John 1:12).

To my big, wonderful family, with special thanks to Robert for affirming my achievements before I earn them, to Bettina, for your loving interest in every detail, and to Beth, for your generous excitement over this book.

To my smart, gifted, ever-faithful friend, the talented Robin Joss, for exceeding the boundaries of friendship by patiently listening, praying, and strategizing with me. To "little Vanessa" Delgado, for twenty years of loving and faithful assistance.

To the incomparable Eva Marie Everson and Taryn Souders, Word Weavers International, for your exhaustive efforts to create and sustain the Florida Christian Writers Conference, which gave me the opportunity to connect—and the courage to persevere.

To my Page 33 writer's critique group of award-winning, multi-published writers Lori, Jean, Julie, Lisa, Jeannie, and Alissa, you've critiqued much of this manuscript, cheered my blessings, and dried my tears through every little setback. You've helped me grow as an author and as a woman of God.

To my close friends near and far, how I wish I could thank each of you by name for faithfully praying for me and forgiving my lack of attention. I thank God for you. Thank you, Laurie Farquhar, for opening resources, RoseAnn Lovell for celebrating me, and Diane Klumb, Dottie Wobb, Carol Getty, Jane Cruickshanks, Sandra Kinder, and my Bible study friends for supporting me with so much prayer and love.

Elizabeth Brickman is a compassionate expert in the world of financial advising and spiritual wellness. Better known as The Caring Advisor, Elizabeth is also a multi-award-winning author whose new series will change readers' lives. As a wealth-confident woman in a profession dominated by male voices, Elizabeth adds a unique perspective that enriches hearts as well as portfolios.

Through her writing, speaking, blogging, and The Caring Advisor podcast, which has reached audiences around the world, Elizabeth offers a distinctive approach to wealth. She helps her audience develop the inner resources of high achievers by tapping into God's power to grow their financial and relational lives with confidence and Christ-centered happiness. Her spiritual insights are rich, loving, and light-hearted.

A former, nationally recognized, award-winning financial advisor and president of her Registered Investment Advisory firm, Elizabeth has a proven track record of success. For twenty-five years, she served private clients from every walk of life in eighteen states. She was regularly quoted in the nationally syndicated financial press and was a periodic guest on Business Financial News radio.

As a Certified Kingdom Advisor, Elizabeth is credentialed to provide financial counsel from a biblical worldview.

Elizabeth offers a much-needed perspective, connecting finance to emotional and spiritual wellness. Her style is engaging, approachable, and fun. She motivates her readers to achieve victorious breakthroughs via innovative, faith-based strategies.

Elizabeth loves her life in sunny South Florida with her beloved husband of over thirty years and her pet orchid, Ophelia. Elizabeth is happiest when tucked in her home library, cappuccino in hand, reading, writing, thinking, and praying.